Eduard Beltran is a lawyer, consultant, university professor (Institut d'Etudes Politiques de Paris and Universidad Complutense de Madrid) and expert in leadership and negotiation.

Eduard has trained more than 10,000 professionals in more than 40 countries on 5 continents. He is the managing director of the Center for Negotiation (CEFNE). He is a graduate of the Institut d'Etudes Politiques de Paris, also holds a law degree from the University of Barcelona, a Master in International Law from the University of Barcelona, a Master in International Law (LLM) from New York University (NYU) and is an alumni of the École Nationale d'Administration (ENA), Simone Veil promotion.

Eduard is the author of "*The Secret Art of Negotiation*", Plataforma Publishing House, July 2020.

The author could be reached by email: contact@emerit-publishing.com.

© Emerit Publishing – June 2021

ISBN 978-2-35940-027-4
97, rue Nollet
75017 Paris
http:///www.emerit-publishing.com

Eduard Beltran

# *Leadership*
# The positive influence

*Guide & Methodology*

*Develop your own leadership with tools, techniques and concrete examples with which you can meet challenges and prepare for the management transformations of the post-COVID era.*

*Foreword:*
Olivier Charmeil,
Executive Vice-President SANOFI, General Medecine

# FOREWORD

Twenty-five years of corporate responsibility have led me to reflect a lot as a practitioner on leadership, compared to the first ideas I had when I started my career. The role and place of leaders have evolved considerably in companies in recent years. While leadership continues to be defined as the ability to influence and coach members of a group, the attributes of a good leader have changed.

The topic of leadership was little discussed when I was a young student in business school; most of the attention at that time was focused on strategy. Today, the central question is less the question of strategy than the question of its implementation. And therefore, this leads implicitly to the question of leadership to ensure the execution of the strategy.

I learned about leadership on the job, learning from my own mistakes but also from the great bosses I had the chance to work with. Compared to the vision I had at the beginning of my career, where the leader was simply defined as the chief, the experience quickly taught me that the good leader is an individual capable of managing teams, not vertically and hierarchically by using the classic mechanisms of recognition and sanction in an alternative way, but with an open personality capable of developing horizontal ecosystems.

As Eduard Beltran points out, the good leader is the one who is able to create the vision, to articulate it before communicating it. He is stimulated by uncertainties and ambiguities, resolutely optimistic and more inclined to see the world from the side of opportunities than to suffer from its constraints. He is the one who is able to bring in external perspectives to better integrate them. He is not on the path of optimization, he seeks to transform, he is resolutely oriented towards the future and is able to get out of the myopia of the past. My personal experience quickly made me understand that the good leader is the one who is able to project himself, unlike the manager who manages the existing. It is easier to be a good manager than a great leader. Great bosses taught me that good leaders are more interested in taking ten steps forward than one step. They know the difference between what is urgent and what is important. All of them were systematically convinced that the recipes of the past have little chance of making the successes of tomorrow. I have always dreamed of being the leader who sees an opportunity in every difficulty. Easier said than done.

Above all, I have learned that the great leader is the one who listens, learns from others and feeds from his discussions with others to better share them. He knows how to waste his time first because he knows he can learn from any situation. One of my first bosses systematically asked his assistant to block out a third of his time, which he used for chance meetings. As Eduard Beltran states in his book, the good leader is resolutely inclusive, empathetic, and believes in diversity in all its forms as a vehicle for excellence. They are part of the team and always seek to empower them. He puts himself resolutely at the service of the group. My best bosses were rarely the best technicians, but they knew above all how to delegate and were convinced that the decisions taken closest to the field were the most effective. A good boss encourages risk-taking and knows that you learn a lot from your failures. My personal experience has taught me that it is by analyzing failures that we can forge the successes of tomorrow.

If strategic coherence is key to the success of any collective human enterprise, one of the essential functions of the leader lies in his ability to surround himself by creating complementary teams. The good leader is first and foremost the one who knows how to build his or her teams to carry out a given project, starting with the key positions that are necessary for the company's success. My best bosses were those who were the most disciplined, spending 80% of their time on strategic issues and choosing people. In the second part of my career, I learned that failures come less from the individuals chosen than from the poor fit between the individuals and the positions they were offered. Beyond choosing teams, one of the most important roles of the leader is to create an environment that allows each person to realize his or her full potential, so that he or she can give the best of him or herself. The good leader has a dynamic vision of his or her teams and is constantly seeking to develop them.

Everyone has their own image of the ideal boss. Mine is, like Eduard Beltran, that of an inspiring boss, nourished by a strong raison d'être that gives coherence to his commitment. He knows that beyond its own objectives, an organization is inspired and guided by something beyond itself. He gives coherence and perspective where it is difficult to give. He is comfortable with making radical decisions that create meaningful change. He forces alignment, the absence of which results in high dysfunctional costs. He has no tolerance for deviant behavior, is guided by a strong sense of integrity and has a true sense of values.

Eduard Beltran will agree with me that the absolute leader does not exist, it is the circumstances that make a leader great. Depending on the company's stage of maturity, the characteristics of the right leader for the circumstances may change. The leader in a growth phase may not have the same profile as the one needed in a redeployment phase. In the same way, the natural leader is not always the best one to ensure the effectiveness of the collective action. There is no leader without a particular situation or issue.

Beyond the exhaustive census of the characteristics of leadership that he conducts with great dexterity, the contribution of Eduard Beltran is multiple given the diversity of his professional experiences lawyer, university professor and expert in negotiation in different cultural backgrounds which gives him a particular depth of field. His contribution is twofold. He confirms that one is not born a leader but that one becomes one by acquiring a good understanding of situations and a good ability to listen, but above all by developing a good degree of self-confidence, which is essential for inspiring authentic trust. Only this confidence can inspire and embrace large teams. He reminds us with great accuracy of the importance of the

*Leadership: the positive influence*

human dimension in leadership and more specifically that leadership is a discipline, an attitude structured around authenticity, humility and consistency. He brings a lot by the pragmatic advice he gives that we want to put into practice.

Olivier Charmeil
Executive Vice President SANOFI, General Medicine

# TABLE OF CONTENT

- INTRODUCTION ARE LEADERS BORN OR MADE? ................ 15
- WHAT IS LEADERSHIP? ................................................... 29
  1. LEADERSHIP: A DEFINITION ........................................ 29
  2. TODAY'S LEADERSHIP: THE NEW LEADERSHIP .............. 42
- THE LEADER IN YOU ..................................................... 53
  1. CONFIDENCE IN ONESELF AND IN OTHERS ................... 53
  2. THE CHARISMA AND MAGNETISM OF THE LEADER ........ 75
  3. PHYSICAL AND MENTAL PREPARATION ....................... 87
  4. CREATE YOUR OWN BRAND ....................................... 95
- THE LEADER AND THE OTHERS ................................... 104
  1. THE LEADER'S ENVIRONMENT .................................. 104
  2. EMPATHY ............................................................. 114
  3. INFLUENCE ........................................................... 120
  4. COMMUNICATION ................................................. 128
  5. COOPERATION / LEADERSHIP TEAMS ....................... 138
- THE LEADER AND THE COMPANY ............................... 147
  1. VISION, STRATEGY AND TACTICS ............................ 147
  2. CUSTOMER ORIENTATION ...................................... 158
  3. RISKS AND DECISION MAKING ................................ 165
  4. VALUE CREATION, PROBLEM SOLVING AND INNOVATION .......... 176
- CONCLUSION ............................................................. 193
- BIBLIOGRAPHY .......................................................... 203
- ACKNOWLEDGEMENTS ............................................... 209

# INTRODUCTION

# INTRODUCTION
# ARE LEADERS BORN OR MADE?

> *"Talent does not exist. Talent is having the desire to do something."*
> Jacques Brel

Leadership is the ability of a person to influence and influence is everywhere: from politics to business, from civil society to our family, from the ancient world to the post-Covid era. But what exactly does leadership mean? What does it mean to be a good leader today? Are good leaders made or born leaders? What can you do to prepare or improve your leadership journey?

The 15 chapters of this book answer all of these key questions and address many more issues related to the notion of leadership, especially in business. Through these pages, we will help you work on developing your skills so that you learn the techniques and tools that will make you a successful leader, both professionally and personally.

You will find specific concepts, techniques and tools that will guide and assist you through the process of learning to be an effective leader. Remember, you are not a leader just because you want to be a leader, but you are a leader because others recognize you as a leader.

In the course of this book, you will learn, among other things, how to:
- Develop new skills and competences to influence others in a positive way.
- Identify the keys that the leader must take into account, in order to find his or her vision and achieve it.
- Know the key skills of a leader.
- Identify the work routines characteristic of a leader.
- Improve communication with your team and your interlocutors.
- Achieve your goals by motivating your team and your environment

Before we even begin this discovery, we can throw a question in the air: why is leadership so important? Leadership has existed in all societies since the beginning of time. But today we find this word everywhere. I am sure that several answers will come to your mind, and they will all be very specific. In any case, we know that we need leadership. Throughout this book, we will learn the why of leadership and what has happened in our society to make the need for leaders in all areas increasing.

Leadership is now a necessary skill for any professional who wants to shine and succeed in their projects. We can choose not to develop our leadership, but in that case, we must accept that our career and success will not be the same.

Traditionally, the way to get others do things was based on two rather blunt techniques, the so-called "carrot or stick" technique. I could motivate people in essentially two ways, by rewarding them or punishing them:

- *"If you succeed, I'll give you a carrot, I'll raise your salary, I'll give you a promotion, I'll give you a better job etc."*
- or *"if you do it wrong"*: I'll hit you with the cane, I'll lower your salary, I'll hit you or I'll throw you out etc.

These are the two motivational techniques that have always been known. However, these two techniques are no longer effective today for three reasons.

First, we realized that financial or economic conditions have less and less impact on people in favor of other motivations (quality of life, career prospects etc.). For example, for the "millennial" generation, the primary motivation is no longer money, but rather work-life balance, flexibility in work, fulfillment rather than success, a mission, a meaning, values etc.

Secondly, applying the carrot and stick technique with people who work with us internally is possible and we can do it, but we cannot use this technique with people with whom we have no direct power, we cannot talk like this with our customers, or with our suppliers because it makes no sense and has no future.

So, we need to look at other types of techniques to motivate and look for other techniques to influence people to go in the direction we want.

Third, today we find more and more companies and institutions that have a more transversal (horizontal) structure, leaving behind the traditional pyramidal structure (boss-employee, called top-down). Before, in most organizations, people had a boss and, underneath, there was a team that worked under them. Today, we find many companies in which no one has a "boss" or "team", workers have more and more autonomy and equal conditions in front of their interlocutors within the company itself (transversal structure). This has been further amplified with teleworking since the Covid crisis of 2020.

For this new paradigm, we need a set of tools, techniques and methods that allow us to influence people to go our way and without the need to use the outdated technique of stick or carrot (punishment or reward).

Leadership is a very necessary skill that complements you as a professional; regardless of the discipline and your industry, whether internal or external, you will have to influence. Traditionally, there was a misconception that leadership was only applicable internally within a company. Today, we know that a good leader is not only a good leader inside the company, but also outside, because if you are not able to motivate your own suppliers, external partners, stakeholders and customers, you are not a good leader.

Example: let's imagine the President of the French Republic, who has a good leadership in his country, with his collaborators, with the Prime Minister, with the media of his country, with his citizens, but who has no leadership with the other European leaders, the other world leaders, the business leaders, and the international companies present in France. It is obvious that he is a bad leader, because he will only be an internal leader and he will not be able to influence all these people who are important.

The dimension of true leadership has changed. Today we have 360 leaders capable of influencing internally and externally all the actors involved in your projects.

A key question people often ask is whether you are born a leader or have become one?

What we do know, because science has proven it and practitioners have confirmed it, is that leaders are made. Leaders work hard to become leaders. On the basis of learning, training, observation and practice, they manage to become good leaders. As in the end, in any field of life, you have to work hard to get something and finally you learn everything. Not only from our own experience, but also from observing the best, from scientific research and from ourselves. We have analyzed dozens of leaders from different fields of activity, politics, business, sports, culture, etc. All these leaders have several points in common, one of which is undoubtedly key: the will and the permanent capacity to learn and improve.

### *Example of learning in life (even from the best):*

Frank Sinatra, when he was already an established singer and making a living singing in an orchestra in New York, was advised by an artist representative to take private lessons, even though he was already singing well (he already had "the voice"), but the purpose was to practice more and improve his skills, so that he would use his voice better and not get too tired, thus getting a better performance. Years later, Sinatra himself acknowledged that having these private lessons helped him a lot in his career because he sang well, yes, but these lessons gave him techniques and skills that helped him improve.

Another current example is that of Rafael Nadal, a great international tennis player, who, despite being one of the best players in the world, needs a trainer and a coach to motivate him to improve and become a better player.

The example of Steve Jobs' leadership training is also worth thinking about. If you look at an interview, a conference or a speech from the beginning of the 80's they have nothing to do with the Steve Jobs of the 2000's, neither in the aesthetics, nor in the magnetism of the character, nor in the ability to communicate, nor in having his own identity. In the 80's he was a rather shy man with an uncharacteristic style and the 2000's man became a man with a much more charismatic aesthetic with his black turtleneck sweater, his small glasses, his short hair and short beard obtaining a look of confident leader much more powerful, printing his own mark. Steve Jobs worked on himself and his leadership.

There is a phrase from the Belgian singer Jacques Brel that we like a lot and that is "Talent is desire" because when we talk about the talent of the leader, we also refer to the desire of the leader to be a leader.

> *"Leadership and the willingness to learn go together. Leaders learn to be leaders and they continue to learn as leaders."*
> John F Kennedy

A good leader is made because he wants to be a leader, because he is inspired by other leaders and especially because he works on his skills to be one.

## *Leadership: the positive influence*

The leader to be a leader needs only one thing (it seems to be a joke, but it is not): to have followers, because a leader who has all the virtues of a leader (charisma, ability to convince, a great vision) but that nobody follows is not a leader, it is an expert, or it is an interesting interlocutor but it is not a leader. Who is the first to follow a leader? The first one who must follow a leader is himself, that is, the first one who must have a leader is himself. I need to have the power to convince myself that what I am going to do as the leader is right. I need to have confidence in myself, otherwise I will not be able to demand that others have confidence in me.

If we try to synthesize the two key concepts to be a leader, summarizing the great theorists of the field, we can say that leadership can be summarized in two words: vision and empathy.

And knowing what those two words really mean, we could just end this book on leadership here. If you have a vision, you are empathetic, you know where you want to go, you anticipate, you release energy and illusion so that people trust you and follow you, you are already a leader! What we are going to try to do in this leadership book is to go deeper into how we need to do it and propose a method to have a vision and to release empathy.

Without a doubt, leadership is the art of persuasion, the art of having the ability to move people in the direction you want. A true leader knows how to exert a positive influence on others. Leadership is not about power but about social influence on people. You are not a leader because of your status, money or professional position but you are a leader because of the recognition of others.

Leadership has nothing to do with the title of the person, you can be a director, a minister or a president and not have any leadership etc.

No doubt, your future without leadership would be compromised and limited in time.

Leadership is a concept as old as the world itself. Throughout history, leaders have emerged and shaped future leaders for generations to come. Leaders have challenged the "status quo," emerged in times of great crisis, helped to overcome moments of change, and generated movements of people as followers.

What leaders have in common, it seems, is a deep level of awareness. This is accompanied by a great ability to understand their environment and to inspire others to follow them. It is relentlessly expressed in their ability to execute and achieve their goals. We will analyze in detail the concept of leadership and leader which has its roots in looking within, influencing around, building and achieving one's vision.

You don't have to be in a certain position to be a leader. A project or area manager can influence the people on the team he or she leads, yet is not the president of the company. However, not everyone is born with the innate ability (or willingness!) to be a leader even if they are in a leadership position. In this case, you can acquire the skills necessary to become a leader through the in-depth study of leadership through practical techniques and tools that will provide you with everything nature did not give you in this sense. If you don't develop these skills, you will probably become a follower. Even if you are in a position of power, people will not follow you even if they like certain behaviors in you.

In this book, you will learn that the first important skill of a great leader is following. We are all followers in general no matter what role we play. If you already consider yourself a leader you should strive to apply all the skills of a follower, because leaders are both followers and leaders. It may seem like a paradox but great leaders must be followers at the same time. Let's imagine that you are the President of the Republic, you may have a vision for your country but on certain economic, legal or scientific aspects, you will follow experts who are leaders in their field. A bit like Picasso: he probably influenced many artists but he himself was influenced throughout his career by other artists and intellectuals who were leaders in their field.

> *"Those who try to lead people can only do so by following the crowd."*
> Oscar Wilde

As we have said before, there are two essential things that every leader must have:
- First of all, a clear and defined vision of the direction he wants to take, of what he means by objective.
- Second, empathy with the people who must lead and share this vision so that they can participate freely according to their will.

You will also learn how to use your skill development and be assertive in your career. Personal development skills are important at any stage of your career and you will also learn the essential resources to develop others.

The leader's vision is a way of thinking about accountability. All intentions, actions, and results must be viewed through the leader's vision in order to focus the leader's fundamental responsibility on results.

In this book, we will discuss practical rather than theoretical tools that, if implemented immediately, will help you get the recognition you want, by improving the results you want for you and your business.

Remember that you are not a leader because you want to be a leader, but because you are recognized as a leader by others.

In each chapter, we will present you with a series of resources so that you can create your own personalized development plan and guide you through it for your organization, your team and yourself. If you adopt the development techniques we present in this book, your results will improve, your reputation will shine and your career will undoubtedly be boosted.

And finally, you will learn how to motivate those around you to get what you want and that they will want too.

We can only wish you success and happiness in your new life as a leader!

# CHAPTER I

# WHAT IS LEADERSHIP?

# WHAT IS LEADERSHIP?

## 1. Leadership: a definition

- Definition of leadership: the ability to influence people around us to achieve a goal.
- Characteristics of the leader.
- What leaders do compare to managers.
- Some examples of historical leaders: Winston Churchill, Martin Luther King, Nelson Mandela

*"A true leader doesn't have to lead, he just has to show the way."*
Henry Miller

If you go to Google and search for "definition of leadership", you will probably find as many definitions of leadership as there are leaders. The concept of leadership is vast and complex, and has probably been well studied and worked on for centuries. There are many books on the subject, and many different approaches to the concept; Harvard University [1] quotes the existence of over 15,000 books on leadership. The reality is that there are many types of leadership: family, professional, political, religious, etc. and basically everyone has their own definition, but if we were to give a more concrete definition of leadership, we would focus on this idea that the leader is someone who has a vision, who is able to anticipate the future and who empathizes enough with people to make them follow him.

Basically, we can define a leader as someone who is able to influence the people around him to achieve the goal he has set. To speak of leadership is to speak of influence. Leadership is, has been and will be an influence. If we look at the history of the great world leaders from an economic, social and family point of view, they are people who have been able to influence their environment to move in a certain direction.

Very often, this definition of leadership takes all its value when this leader is confronted with a crisis situation. Thus, the leader is defined by what he does and not by what he says.

As we have already noted, leaders are made, not born leaders. They are built with effort and hard work, but then: how can you become a leader? Without a doubt: by training, by reading and learning this discipline, by acquiring the necessary techniques that will allow you to develop these skills of influence etc. and by practicing! Leadership is also a verb; leadership is doing things!

---

[1] Michael Shinagel's 2013 article, The Paradox of Leadership

*Leadership: the positive influence*

"The eminent Master is careful not to speak / And when his work is done and his task is fulfilled / The people say: *this is from me*." Lao Tzu

Leaders have in common a deep level of awareness. This is combined with a great ability to understand their environment and to inspire others to follow them.

In this chapter, we intend to analyze the concept of leadership which is based on looking in, influencing around, and building and executing your vision.

To use the definition, we have been working on throughout this section, leadership is a set of skills that are used to influence the way others think or act, but this term should not focus on anything other than the idea of changing mindsets. Because the leader has the ability to take the initiative and bring innovative ideas, without giving orders.

Nor does leadership mean an unequal distribution of power. And even if the leader has the final say, it is teamwork that produces the best results. As an African proverb says: "If you want to go fast, walk alone. If you want to go far, walk with others". The leader wants to go far rather than walk fast.

We can therefore summarize that leadership is also known as a set of managerial skills, which a person has to influence the way of acting or being, of individuals or group of individuals in a given work, motivating this team to collaborate with enthusiasm to achieve the objective of all its goals and activities.

In addition, leadership is defined as the ability to manage, observe, initiate, convene, promote, motivate, encourage and evaluate a project efficiently and effectively, whether for personal, professional or institutional purposes.

A leader's job is to try to set a goal and get the majority of people to want and work towards that goal. This is essential in the professional and business environment, but also applies to other very different contexts such as education (teachers getting their students to agree with their way of thinking), sports (having the ability to lead the team to success) and even the family environment (in many cases, parents are held up as an example for their children).

Since leadership is the function of a person who stands out from the rest and is able to make good decisions for the group, team or organization that precedes him/her, inspiring the rest of the participants in that group to achieve a common goal, it is also said that leadership involves more than one person: the one who leads (the leader) and those who support him/her (the followers) and enable him/her to develop his/her position effectively.

> *"Leadership is the ability to transform a vision into reality."*
> Warren BENNIS

The role of the leader is to set a goal and get most people to want it and work towards it. We emphasize this idea, but it is essential and fundamental to understanding leadership. In all the areas mentioned above, we were talking about formal leaders, but we can also talk about informal leaders, that is, those who emerge naturally or spontaneously within a group. In any case, the most widespread classification is the one that refers to the link between the leader and the subjects he/she influences (i.e., his/her followers).

A lot of literature and scientific research has tried to classify the types of leaders in several categories. We distinguish three basic types of leadership that we will develop throughout this book: democratic, authoritarian and liberal, and we will now only comment on them.

The democratic leader is the one who, first of all, encourages debate and discussion within the group. Then, he takes into account the opinions of his followers and only then, on the basis of explicit criteria and evaluation standards, makes a decision.

The authoritarian leader, on the other hand, is the one who decides alone, without consultation and without justifying himself to his followers. This type of leader uses one-way communication (no dialogue) with the collaborator or follower.

As for the liberal leader, he usually plays a passive role and cedes power to his group. This is why he does not judge the contribution of the members. He gives them the greatest freedom of action.

Regardless of the leadership style, the basic principles of a good leader are: to keep abreast of the latest developments in the field, to observe the work of other leaders and to change the way he or she works if necessary. On the other hand, the qualities that a leader must possess are: knowledge, confidence, integrity and, of course, a certain charisma to inspire his followers.

The best leaders are those who are visionary, who are able to understand productive situations for the company before they arise, who are innovative and favorable to change. We can take as an example Bill Gates, a student who dropped out of Harvard, but thanks to his leadership qualities, vision and ability to influence, he was able to found one of the most important companies in the technology sector, Microsoft, and thanks to the decisions he was able to take and the trust he obtained from international companies, he became the richest person in the world. He was able to understand that computers would one day become an indispensable part of the home, and he worked to develop the products that would make this possible, he is a good example of a visionary leader.

But it is not enough to have a good idea to become a leader, we must know how to realize it and convince those around us that this idea is the best invention ever imagined and that it aims to solve our most important problems. If we manage to captivate the public with our idea, we can become a visionary leader appreciated by those around us.

Leadership is the key to making a company, department or project work in the field. However, finding people who can successfully develop leadership skills within a team is not an easy task. Many problems stem from a lack of knowledge or different views on the definition of leadership. To give an example, is a good leader based on motivation or results?

To answer this question and establish a realistic concept of a leader, you will learn more below about the importance, styles, skills and myths that exist around this controversial etc. and desired figure.

The importance of leadership is more than evident in many areas of life, even beyond running a business as the leader is responsible for achieving goals in a much more efficient and timely manner.

Leadership is not flat, and depending on the context in which it develops, it can determine the type of social transformation it is capable of. It therefore has a function within the organization, community or society that is distinguished by its relevance and influence.

This is how organizations depend on leadership to grow and endure, and this is where its great importance lies. A leader will be able to establish good communication and improve the integration capacity of the members, all in order to achieve a common goal.

Leadership can also be interpreted as a way of being, a way of leading and how things are shaped over time. It is a process of interaction between members of a group interested in the progress of the organization they work for.

In short, the importance of leadership lies in the fact that it is the key to the survival of any organization. Even more so if we take into account that the ability to guide and lead is at the heart of it.

For example, an organization may have optimal control, proper planning and quality resources, but it will not survive without a leader who is up to the task.

In summary, to conclude this chapter, leadership is above all marked by the context and the situation in which we find ourselves. It can result from different circumstances and events that have taken place. Leadership never comes out of nowhere; the essence of leadership is contextual and is determined by people or events. It is fundamental to examine the context in which a person can become a leader to properly define and understand leadership.

### *What leaders do in relation to managers*

In general, there is some confusion between the concepts of manager and leader.

An interesting definition or analogy that we like to use in our trainings is to say that "a good manager is a good army general in peacetime and a good leader is a good army general in wartime".

Who will be the best general then? It is obvious that the best general in the army is the one who is able to be a good general in peacetime as well as in wartime!

This means that there is a very strong link between management and leadership, we can say that the manager is the person who manages what is on the table, that is to say, he is the one who manages what is established in the contract: he manages people, resources, budgets, the agenda etc. If there is nothing unexpected, the manager can be a manager from the beginning to the end of his professional life. When does the leader figure appear? The leader appears at the moment when something unexpected, out of contract, is born. At that moment, the manager no longer reacts to this situation because he is not trained or prepared for it because he may lack the vision to react correctly and motivate the troops in the right direction.

This is why we associate, perhaps misleadingly, leadership in moments of crisis and/or situations of change, because in a normal situation it is not necessary to be a leader. You can be a perfect manager of your company, of your team as long as there are no abnormal situations.

For example: you are the manager of a restaurant and you are responsible for 10 cooks and 40 servers. In a normal situation, you can manage your team well but imagine that, for example, there is a crisis due to a health epidemic in the whole country (like with Covid 19 in 2020), you have to close the restaurant and we are only allowed to do home deliveries. In this crisis situation, the manager should be a leader to adapt to this new situation and look for solutions! Maybe he could propose that the 10 cooks continue to be cooks, proposes that out of the 40 waiters, some of them dedicate themselves to the reception, others to help in the kitchen and some others to advertise online to attract new customers to this new way of working.

Most of the literature we find on leadership makes a clear difference between leaders and managers. Leaders should invest their time and energy in defining the vision or direction of the organization. They should put all their effort and commitment into aligning resources to convey the realization of that vision and try to be active role models to inspire and motivate by example.

It is important to know the difference between a manager and a leader, because the two concepts are often confused and yet necessary and complementary!

- Manager: it is the person in charge of managing and executing the different elements that are "on the table" to find solutions and to be able to advance the project in which we are.
- Leader: it is the person who emerges at the moment when there is a problem or a difficulty, whether it is budget, human team or context, economic, social or health crisis, etc. And this cannot be developed with the elements that are on the table. He or she will have the vision of where to go and will find the idea of how to get there. He or she will find the solutions that are not written down.

In short, we could say that the manager is the person who follows and respects the rules and the leader is the one who creates and writes them.

> *"Effectiveness is doing things right; efficiency is doing the right things. A manager must be efficient and effective."*
> Peter Drucker

It is also important that the leader we are looking for is the right one.

To become or find the ideal leader of the company, we must look for a person who tries to resemble as much as possible an ideal leader, which would be the one who possesses the following traits:

- Knows how to manage complexity: has the ability to assess the complexity of different situations before obtaining some of the information to be received. His/her actions in complicated situations and decision making in rapidly changing systems are effective and appropriate.
- This leader has a global mentality: every leader must have integrated the ability to recognize what is around us to be able to identify and compare the offers and opportunities of other markets, in order to achieve a global approach of what is happening and developing around him.
- They act strategically with flexibility: strategy has always been an element that all leaders needed to possess. Now, flexibility is an essential element because we need a more continuous and

flexible process, in the short term, because of the world we are facing.
- They promote innovation: monotony and uniformity of strategies, tactics, dispositions etc. are to be avoided, otherwise society will stagnate and we will not progress and advance as a society. No matter how useful these strategies or tactics were in the past or how good they were, they cannot last and serve us forever. Constant renewal is necessary if the goal is to continue to grow and improve.

The pandemic of Covid in 2020 has shown us that we are permanently in a situation of crisis, of change. Today there is no political or economic leader who is able to predict how the year will end because a thousand things can happen throughout the year and despite this, the leader must face all these new unforeseen events that occur.

Examples of three particularly inspiring historical leaders:

### *Winston Churchill (1874-1965)*

He is considered one of the greatest world leaders who ever lived. Churchill, the former British Prime Minister, is known for his ability to inspire, motivate and morally encourage an entire nation during World War II, and it is because of his eloquence. He is considered a stubborn, obstinate, somewhat strange person with a multitude of hobbies, but also an optimistic and positive leader. He had a great sense of humor that made him shine even in really complicated situations.

His self-confidence, perseverance and communication skills characterized him to become a great leader. Through his radio speeches, he was able to motivate, encourage, and inspire hope so that the country would find the strength to continue fighting when it was on the edge of the cliff.

### *Martin Luther King (1929-1968)*

The legacy of this leader who transformed America lives on. Through the article "The Lessons of Martin Luther King", three main lessons served as a manual for all those who want to aspire to be leaders.

First, demonstrating an absolute commitment to a cause is essential to its success. Often, professionals fail because they are unable to make the necessary sacrifices in their personal and professional lives for this commitment.

The second lesson is one that recommends breaking with established beliefs and innovating to achieve change. These actions will often be unpopular, as organizations resist change. However, it is necessary to ask ourselves why we do what we do and do things differently in order to develop and grow.

The third of his virtues was communication. Luther King had a dream, but he could not have realized it if he had not been able to communicate it to everyone around him. Turning the dream into action, convincing others to join him, is the only way to make it come true.

*Leadership: the positive influence*

### *Nelson Mandela (1918-2013)*

Mandela's passing was a blow to millions of people who were inspired by his activism. Mandela was not a perfect guy, but he had a lot of empathy and dealt with essentially personal issues with great transparency. Mandela's patience is one of his traits as a leader, for example, waiting for opportunities and demonstrating his long-term vision. Mandela spent 27 years in prison and took another five years to win the election. Only then did he raise the two fists of defiance that made him the leader not only of the black race, but of all citizens of the world.

The ability to forgive, which when he transferred to the professional environment meant accepting the mistakes of others, earned him the loyalty of those who worked alongside him. He learned from his mistakes and was careful and generous. In addition, he had excellent negotiation skills, which led him to reach agreements in which everyone felt like a winner.

## 2. Today's leadership: the new leadership

- How the world has changed: fourth industrial revolution, permanent crisis, new powers, new generations
- New leader attributes: today's leader is different
- New leaders, new values

*"In matters of style, swim with the current; in matters of principle, stand like a rock."*
Thomas Jefferson

How the world has changed: fourth industrial revolution, permanent crisis, new powers, new generations:

In this chapter, we will first talk about how the world has changed. It is clear that the connectivity between technology, the internet, and biology has led us to a new paradigm, which since 2015 has been called the Fourth Industrial Revolution.

This fourth industrial revolution, also known as Industry 4.0, is the most important industrial milestone known since the beginning of the industrial revolution in the 18th century. The fusion of technologies, some of which are currently in full development, is the most important feature it possesses, crossing the boundaries between the spheres of biology, physics and technology.

In other words, this revolution is the perfect union of technology and biology. For example, driving a car is something that we will soon not have to do, but there is something that is human and that consists of telling the car, in this case, where we are going, in what direction we want to go. The technology will be able to calculate how far we are going to go, how long it will take us to get there, how much fuel we are using, etc. But the command, the destination must be given by a person, in this case it would be the leader. Just as negotiation can never be entrusted to a machine. Why not? Because when we talk about leadership and negotiation, we are talking about searching for information, managing emotions, communicating, managing cultural differences and this, by nature, is purely human. Technology can help us to define and calculate all sorts of parameters except where we want to go, only the leader knows and will decide. In a way, this famous fourth industrial revolution, legitimizes more than ever the leader of today, and the leader of tomorrow.

We add to this fourth industrial revolution all the economic, social and environmental consequences of the Covid pandemic that has hit the world since 2020.

It is true that we are currently in a state of permanent crisis. We understand the concept of crisis as: "a serious and decisive situation that endangers the development of a problem or a process". In any crisis situation, the figure of the leader seems essential, in a way the crisis makes the leader emerge.

If we look back, we can ask ourselves if General de Gaulle or Winston Churchill would have been the leaders, they were without the existence of World War II, when they had the opportunity to emerge as leaders out of necessity. Without that war we would probably not see them as the leaders we see them today throughout history.

There are events that push you to be a leader and today we are talking about a state of permanent crisis. Just stop and think about the history of the early 20th century. If you take that stage between 2000 and today, we've had three huge crises: the 9/11 attacks, the financial crisis of 2008, and the coronavirus health crisis in 2020. These three elements constitute a new world in which the situation of crisis and change is constant, whether it be due to terrorist attacks, financial crises, health crises, environmental disasters, etc.

New powers have emerged that we did not imagine before, not only geopolitically, but also in terms of new multilateral organizations, very powerful multinational corporations, the media and at the individual level. To quote a recent example, the emergence of the Swedish environmental activist Greta Thunberg shows us how a person with 15 years and no economic structure behind her became a leader and, in general, made this concept of leadership much more complex and diversified.

Today's world is different from the one we knew before, it is a much more complex world; legally, technically, financially, socially complex, etc.

If we think of the actors of influence, they are multiple: from the more state-based actors such as governments and national entities, to large multinationals, to religious leaders, to leaders by industry, and even to the relatively anonymous leaders of social movements, who are not sure who is behind them like the Black Blocks. This is a complex environment that is leading us to a new leadership.

The new generations of professionals and people, such as the so-called Z generation (people born between 1997 and 2010), have a different way of approaching things than the one other generation are used to. Their approach will certainly be in line with the new times we are going to live in, but in any case, we have to adapt to this new generation that has come and gone, because the generations to come will be much closer to the generation that lived through the technological change in the first place than to the one that lived through the fall of the Berlin Wall or the emergence of the Internet.

### *New Leader Attributes: Today's leader is different:*

This new concept of today's leader perhaps indicates that he or she must be a more trained, more informed, more technological, more open to the media, more immediate, more international, more multicultural leader. All this means that today's leader has needs that did not exist before, for example, Julius Caesar, Alexander the Great, Abraham Lincoln, surely had different qualities and characteristics than Kamala Harris, Elon Musk or Greta Thunberg.

It is clear that the environment shapes the corporate world as much as the corporate world today shapes the world at large. By extension, corporate leadership has also been shaped by many current influences and crises.

Society has moved away from what is collective and has consolidated a culture oriented towards the individual, which affects both the way of producing and the way of marketing and managing.

These changes have an impact on all components of work and business management, on leadership style, strategy, processes, personnel management, production and technological systems, marketing, organizational structure, competitiveness and efficiency criteria, as well as the impact of companies on society.

As determinants of the new leadership style, we have:
- Treatment "person to person", "equal to equal", in the relationship with others.
- Positive treatment of the other person, resulting in an effective outcome for both parties: win-win.
- "Non-manipulative" treatment oriented towards the common good of both parties, generating a fruitful long-term relationship.
- Possibility of positively and effectively influencing all areas of activity (customers, suppliers, employees, partners, etc.). Notion of cooperation or partnership.

It is necessary that the leader knows how to create visions that mobilize the will and behavior of himself and others. Through vision, we can motivate people to act of their own free will and thus change their behavior.

To achieve this, it is necessary to know what is important to them, what they value, what they need, how much time they have, etc.

Finally, today's leader must not only manage change, but also start from change. To achieve this, he or she must be aware of the major challenges of the world. Being constantly informed and having access to reliable information is undoubtedly a prerequisite for today's leader.

Today, the leader-coach model is fashionable in companies; but we cannot imagine, for example, that Napoleon leads his army on the battlefield while he asks his generals for their opinion, listens to them patiently, asks them questions, gets information, creates a link with them etc. And all this while his soldiers fight and die, confident that their leader will find the appropriate tactics according to the evolution of events.

Fortunately, we are not in that situation in today's world and the leader-coach model is gaining ground in companies, especially when it can be anticipated and prepared.

Analyzing history, this should not be a surprise either because it is a direct and natural consequence of human evolution, which Maslow explained so well with his famous pyramid. If, after a war, the most important thing is to survive, we are at the base of the pyramid and here, daily life is worthwhile: to be able to eat, to have a roof under which to sleep and not to freeze to death in winter. At the other end of the pyramid, at the top, is personal fulfillment. Between the two extremes is evolution, the path of people towards their own development and, consequently, that of society. Once the basic needs, mentioned above, are met, stability is then sought through employment, family, health, etc.; from there, progression in self-development through integration into related groups and feeling different from the rest of the people: soccer teams, social clubs, professional associations. From this need of integration and belonging to a group begins the path of uniqueness. It is no longer enough to belong to a social group, a work team, etc., but to want to stand out and seek recognition and respect from others. Finally, the individual achieves his or her own realization. His self-esteem no longer depends on others, because he gives himself to himself. He esteems and respects himself and this "non-dependence" on the opinion and appreciation of others is what makes him, in the end, free and therefore fulfilled.

New leaders: new values. Ex: Elon Musk, Kamala Harris, Greta Thunberg

Where is the Western world after 70 years without world wars? Because after years of climbing the ladder of development, the people of our business world are at the penultimate stage, where they need to be recognized and respected for their uniqueness.

To name a few new leaders, we would mention Elon Munsk, a great technology leader, a great anticipator of future needs, also Kamala Harris, a vice president with a very different way of communicating, listening, reacting, very close to the people and finally, we have already mentioned her before, Greta Thunberg. She is someone who has practically no experience because of her young age and who has no commercial or institutional structure behind her, who appears with no prior legitimacy but whose timing and speech fit perfectly and make a leader emerge. This indicates that basically anyone in an ideal situation can become a leader.

What do these three leaders have in common? They have a very powerful brand image, a very direct communication image, a very strong presence in the media and social networks and an ability to adapt to a discourse and desire that the public expects.

It is said that in order to know how to love, one must first know how to love oneself. In the same way, to be a leader, you must know how to lead yourself.

These are the leaders of today. These are the leaders that companies are looking for, for their positions of responsibility in this fourth industrial revolution of the post Covid era.

# CHAPTER II

# THE LEADER IN YOU

# THE LEADER IN YOU

## 1. Confidence in oneself and in others

- Know yourself/identify your leadership style
- Self-confidence (confidence versus fear), the concept of vulnerability
- Inspire trust: authenticity, logic and empathy (the Triangle of Trust)

> *"If you have confidence in yourself, you will inspire confidence in others."*
> H. W. Arnold

*Confidence in self and others:*

Today, we are in constant debate about how we can "be better", what really makes us happy and how we can add value to our lives and especially to our professional careers. There is something inside us that "screams" that we are capable of more, that we can be better people and that we can do many different things. The problem is knowing where to look, where to find it and then how to use that to become a good leader.

Leadership is a way of facing and approaching life. It is born out of the need to understand and respond in today's world and is a thinking of who I am, what I believe and what I do. As we said in the first chapter of this book, there are almost as many definitions of leadership as there are leaders, even if we ask ten different people what leadership means to them, we will most likely get ten different definitions. We may have overlooked the fact that meaning and importance emerge within us, the first step to being a leader to others is to be a leader to myself, one must be their first follower.

It is important to understand that before managing and leading others, it is essential to manage ourselves, to become aware of the main dimensions we have as a person and to evaluate whether we should go further or stay the same. No matter how many techniques you are taught to learn to be a leader, if they don't match "who I am", you won't be able to implement them effectively.

*"Yes We Can"*
Barack Obama

However, leadership is not a trait exclusive to some, leadership is something that is worked on and built. These traits that constitute the raw material of a leader can be acquired. Link these characteristics to the desire to be a leader and nothing will stop you from becoming one. No one is exempt from being a leader or a follower. Awakening one's leadership potential is everyone's responsibility and job. In any circumstance, with any type of activity, there is always, always a person who exerts an important and remarkable influence on others.

In today's work environment, the goal of leadership is not the same as in the past. Today, organizations and companies are looking for a leader, not only as someone to follow, but now, in addition, it must be someone who is able to awaken and motivate the development of the emotional skills of others, to create relationships and bonds and who has the ability to guide others in their personal development.

Above all, a leader must be able to lead change and show his followers how to manage change, overcome difficulties and be increasingly adaptable. He or she must know how to direct people's behaviour in order to meet new challenges and improve their ability to learn. To achieve this, the leader must act and work as a guide who understands others and himself.

The leader must help them develop their skills and abilities to achieve the strongest and most enduring commitment to the outcome and the team.

His leadership qualities will determine his level of success and that of those who work with him. He must keep the people who work with him motivated so that they not only do their jobs well, but also do them with all their heart.

At this point, we can list a lot of skills that today's leaders should have, some of them could be:
- self-knowledge,
- influence,
- self-control,
- the ability to resolve conflicts,

- the ability to manage difficulties.

The most important of these skills is that the leader learns to develop them, to implement them and to go within oneself, and then to contribute with our leadership to the group of people he/she will lead.

Once again, we emphasize that most leadership skills can be learned, developed and/or improved. That is why we must first explore ourselves in order to know ourselves and be a leader of ourselves, only in this way will we succeed in being one to others.

*Know yourself/identify your leadership style*

To be a good leader, you need to have the right character and to achieve this, it is important to develop a balanced conscience.

*"Know thyself, and thou shalt know the universe and the Gods."*
Motto of Socrates:
inscription on the threshold of the
temple of Delphi, attributed to Socrates

## 1.1. Gain self-confidence

Every leader needs not only skills and knowledge, but also mental and emotional preparation for new challenges.

Self-confidence is a fundamental aspect and to build it and be able to generate it in others, it is necessary to polish some paradigms and practices that can interfere with your image and performance as a leader.

Companies are increasingly presenting a more horizontal management structure, leaving behind the corporate formalities of twenty years ago. A confident leader must know and learn how to improve his company. To do this, he or she must allow and rely on an effective and timely contribution and exchange of ideas that benefit the rest of the employees.

> *"You have to believe in yourself, that's the secret."*
> Charlie Chaplin

The leader does not impose, the leader pushes, motivates and collaborates to make things happen. It's a role that requires patience and involves many aspects of your emotional and personal life. Because you reflect in your work what you are in your daily life. It is therefore essential to offer your collaborators a close, humble, wise and effective presence so that, in a reciprocal way, you get the same from them. It is very important not to forget direct contact and communication in the age of immediacy.

In the era of social distance caused by the Covid, it is more important than ever to stay close.

Be empathetic, identify with their needs, aspirations and realities. One of the most important keys to being a better leader is to develop empathy in order to know how to introduce stimuli that provoke positive responses.

In the same way, don't resist change and understand that mistakes are also part of the journey and that the most important thing, even if it sounds like a cliché, is to learn from them and make the most of every circumstance. You learn from everything.

> *"Failure is not the opposite of success; it is a part of success."*
> Arianna Huffington

## 1.2. Gain self-confidence (confidence versus fear)

Here is a 7 key points practical guide on how to become a better leader and increase your confidence. Again, we advise you to be understanding in both your life and mind and in the lives and minds of your colleagues.

### 1.2.1. Gain your mind

Learning to increase self-confidence as a leader is a task that begins in the mind. This is where the will resides and must remain firm in the face of the swaying thoughts that arise in every situation.

Mastering awareness and practicing mindfulness will allow us to identify what we need to change in our value system.

The development of our intra-personal intelligence will allow us to recognize ourselves.

That's what being a better leader is all about: understanding what we know and what we don't know. This will allow us to build and strengthen our confidence as a leader and practice our humility to delegate and trust the work of your team. It is positive and necessary to consolidate a dynamic without fear, without distance and with good feedback.

### 1.2.2. Be realistic but not negative

Another of the points to consider to be a better leader is based on the balance between rationality and motivation. We must always avoid the extremes of negativity and excessive optimism. Remember that creativity is important and has more impact when it helps to solve and improve your environment. Although no action is totally perfect, we must not lose confidence or security when doubts and fears assail us because they will almost always be mental illusions.

Ask yourself firmly and forcefully: why not, why not me, and why not now?

The leader transmits his way of thinking, his beliefs and his values to his team.

Therefore, if your perception and action is passive or negative, it will reflect back to your team with indifference and discord. If the behavior persists, we advise you to think about whether you should continue to be the leader. But don't worry, to help you increase your confidence as a leader, follow this advice:

- Think coolly and consider what your team can convey to you, listening to their perspective can help.
- Don't shy away from big challenges, take them as opportunities for growth.
- Avoid denial, as it is possible to negotiate a solution.

### 1.2.3. Be transparent and resolve conflicts

To become a better leader, we must be serious and firm. We must clearly confront what we don't like, what makes us feel weak or uncomfortable. Project a transparent and solid image and you will gain recognition and credibility with it.

Resolve your personal and team concerns to move forward with peace of mind, it is important to keep your mind away from worries and distractions.

We advise you to make a list of personal and professional commitments that you need to attend to in order to better organize yourself. Achieving the perfect balance between your personal life and your work is what you should strive to convey to your team, reconciliation is possible. Maintain the ethics and responsibility with which you accepted the leadership position in the first place.

## 1.2.4. Recognize each other and work as a team

To know how to increase confidence as a leader, you need to be able to admire and recognize the abilities of the other. This will help you reduce the stress of being the one in charge and responsible for everything and will allow for the flow of ideas and the distribution of duties according to each member's ability.

Cooperation helps you exercise your intelligence, self-esteem and confidence as a leader.

Active listening, improving your empathy and being open-minded are essential elements in learning to be a better leader. You will be able to take initiative naturally, identify the emotions implicit in your team's behavior and understand their personal priorities and values. You will be able to unite your team with humility, knowing that you are all equally necessary to achieve the company's goals.

## 1.2.5. Don't try to run away from the error

A strong will is needed to implement the fifth of our recommendations. Because the road to leadership is not only full of good decisions, sometimes mistakes are made. So, when a decision and action do not meet expectations, it is easy for leaders to get into a crisis and become frustrated. A bad decision will not only affect them, but also the team and the company. It is inevitable to feel this way, but what you can avoid is the downtime that occurs immediately afterwards.

A resilient leader is able to see and extract the good from what has seemed bad.

Learning to improve self-confidence as a leader means seeing and understanding failure and error in a different light, because there is no doubt that both are part of everyone's life. We must therefore assume that some parameters will not be controlled or that we do not know how to do it. In this way, we will be able to recognize each other's potential and the next time, the margin of error will be considerably reduced.

You must take risks and responsibilities, your determination as a leader inspires your team.

To be a better leader, we should start by not comparing ourselves to others or putting circumstances in perspective to justify ourselves. On the contrary, the one who is authentic and exposes himself to his team is much more effective, motivating and recognizing them to better integrate and unite their efforts.

## 1.2.6. Keep your emotional balance at bay

The sixth skill that will help you increase your confidence as a leader in this case is to work on your innermost aspects. Mainly, about yourself, you need to maintain consistency between who you are, what you feel and what you say. Because every dimension of the human being is reflected in his communication. So, if your goal is to understand and train yourself on how to be a better leader, start with a self-evaluation.

Work on your emotional intelligence, so you can understand how you feel and what you are transmitting to others.

Learn to identify your own emotions, needs, motivations and impulses and you will learn to see those of others more easily, improving your actions and confidence as a leader. However, remember that this is a tool that must be used in a controlled manner so as not to disturb or embarrass your teammates.

Physical, mental and emotional health improves your confidence and performance as a leader.

## 1.2.7. Be prepared, but also enjoy the journey

There are two aspects that seem far away to be better leaders and they are: preparation and fun. Well, to know how to increase your confidence as a leader, it is equally effective to use both the intellectual and the ability to laugh at yourself. Facilitate the assimilation of the objectives, the reduction of the own and group stress and the frontality in the communication.

*Knowledge is as important as a sense of humor!*

Being a good leader starts when you feel ready to lead your people. This includes knowing how to motivate them and share your personality and feelings with each of them. Improve your self-esteem and willingness to serve and show your team a committed and honestly involved leader. In this way, you will improve your management and see growth and cohesion within your team or company.

## 1.3. Inspire trust: authenticity, logic and empathy

One of the main factors that will likely determine the success or failure of many businesses and professionals is credibility. Having a good reputation is essential to success. Why would we prefer to be treated by a certain doctor rather than another? The answer is that we trust that professional, because he or she has a good reputation, because he or she conveys trust to us. For people to want to follow us, for them to consider including us in their circles and relationships, they must be sure that we are worthy of their trust. In short, that we are credible.

> *"People without credibility and resources often don't get the momentum they need to get their ideas out into the world."*
> Seth Godin

The people with whom we interact will try to find out if you are really telling them the truth and if you are able to keep your word. That's why we must take every opportunity in our communications to show that we are always telling the truth.

In these fast-moving times, where fake news is the order of the day, where leaders say words that no longer correspond to reality and where what is said today will probably have another version tomorrow, we no longer know what to believe, we must work on our credibility.

***Some recommendations to strengthen our credibility:***

Being different from others when we have our own business or profession will not be enough to succeed, attracting public attention and being credible in order to gain trust is what will help us strengthen our image in an increasingly competitive environment.

In this very competitive world, it is important not only to be credible, but also to prove it. The following tools are very important to work on credibility:

## 1.3.1. Your word and your commitment are unquestionable

Commitment must be total during the execution of the work. The easiest way to lose credibility is to not follow through on what you agreed to with your client, supplier or contact. Pay attention to the details, so you don't end up in a default situation, so you don't contribute to reinforcing that image with those who doubt you. Take responsibility and be consistent. Don't make excuses.

*"CHOOSE WHAT YOU DO BEST AND BE PREPARED EVERY DAY"*

### 1.3.2. Be honest

There is no doubt that your credibility will be instantly damaged if you are dishonest. Lying is not a good idea, nor is it an option to consider. You should also not make unwelcome comments or provide information that is of no interest to the other person. When a person is convinced of something, they say it quickly and without delay.

### 1.3.3. Actively listen to others and give them credit

Instead of trying to monopolize conversations, try to learn to listen to others. This will show that you accept the opinions of others in order to improve yourself. Recognizing the merits and progress of others, not just when it is obvious, will help build your credibility and good judgment.

### 1.3.4. 4. Build a network of credible contacts

Build an environment of trusted people that reinforces the idea that you have a serious project. It may be a good idea to introduce your team to experienced people or even use the contacts of friends who can speak well of you to others.

### 1.3.5. Monitor your reputation

No one else is responsible for your behavior. If you do something that damages your reputation, you will immediately jeopardize your project or business and risk being affected. If what you say does not match what others see, you will not be a credible person.

### 1.3.6. Work objectively without getting into unnecessary debates

It's really important that you don't deal with any sensitive topics of discussion that don't belong to your project. Don't waste your time on this, focus all your energy and resources only on the tasks that will help you achieve the goals you have set.

### 1.3.7. Be consistent with what you do and say

Every action has an effect and leaves a mark, every project needs a motivated guide. Be consistent with what you say and what you do, otherwise you will lose credibility. Show that it is possible to achieve the objectives and you will set an example. Punctuality in deadlines, payments and management plays an important role in this.

### 1.3.8. Be humble

We are not born with knowledge about everything. It is likely that at some point we will have to acknowledge our lack of knowledge on a subject. Admit it and comment on it before you venture to give misinformation. A true "I don't know" can do more for your credibility than you think. A truly credible person knows who they are, where they belong and will not try to sound like the person or expert they are not.

### 1.3.9. Be the best

Hone your five senses and bring out the best in everything you do. The only difference between doing well and doing good is wanting to stand out. Be disciplined enough to be motivated, productive and excellent.

You must be the expert in the field you are working on!

Expertise is the best way to influence those around you!

### 1.3.10. Be accountable for your results

There is a balance between personal and professional life, but that is why you must be attentive to the important tasks of the project. No one can take responsibility for your results, attitudes and behavior.

How can we make our partners feel comfortable talking to us and build our credibility?

Below are some suggestions and phrases you can use to make the conversation a success and have the opportunity to build your credibility:

- *"If I may, I will introduce myself. I am etc."*

  It's not about telling your whole CV, the story of your company or your project in 5 to 10 minutes. Simply introduce yourself and tell us who you are, your background, your current situation and what need or problem you are solving briefly. In addition to strengthening our self-confidence, we will gain credibility with our contacts because, thanks to this presentation, they will know better who we are.

- *"I understand."*

  Empathy is a very important trait, because being empathetic will show that we not only care about ourselves, but that we also care a lot about what happens to the people around us. They will feel much more comfortable because they will feel that we care.

- *"The benefits you will find in etc."*

  They need to know what solutions we are going to provide and what added value our proposal offers them.

  If we are in a meeting where we are talking about our professional qualities, we need to make sure that we communicate to our interlocutor how he will benefit from our actions, that is to say what he will get from us. This is very important if you are in a meeting to present a project, a product or your service. You are there to help them and give the best of yourself so that they save money and time, increase their visibility and productivity, improve their brand image, etc.

- *"The data shows that etc."*

    If we can base our claims on statistics, current research, proven data, etc., it will give us credibility and confidence if we want to demonstrate our knowledge on a topic. If you feel that your experience or opinion is not enough to gain the confidence of the person you are speaking to, be sure to present facts, figures and numbers to give strength to your speech.

- *"Yes" or "I will."*

    Not always, but giving an affirmative answer when others are in need and waiting for our help is a very good strategy to gain confidence and succeed in completing a certain project.

    While it won't always be possible, we should avoid answers that show we don't want to do something, such as "I'm very busy, but I'll try," or those in which we show we're not sure how to do the job, such as "I'll see what I can do."

- *"Our results leave no room for doubt."*

    Showing evidence that confirms our good results in previous and similar work is the best showcase we will have to build trust. Learn to recognize the successes of our company and our career. Even the smallest successes can be recognized if they are accompanied by credibility.

- *"I am also concerned about this issue because etc."*

    We need to show the other person that we are up to date on the issues that concern them and be able to explain why it is also in our best interest. If we know and believe that we can do this well without seeming to "suck up" to them, we can share a brief personal story related to the topic at hand.

- *"Thank you."*

    It's good to be grateful. Use simple and polite words of thanks that will help us to evoke positive emotions, build trust, and enhance our credibility. "Thank you for taking the time" "I am very grateful that you came to this meeting/presentation/event" can be examples that show your appreciation.

In short, our communication must make a contribution to:
- Clarity: I make the complex simple.
- Openness: I am available and close.
- Naturalness: I am myself, what you see is what you get.
- Passion: I can connect from emotion.
- Credibility: I inspire confidence and respect in others.
- Humor: I manage to shorten distances.
- Humility: I am not the protagonist.

Credibility is a commitment to working responsibly and professionally, which helps us generate the trust needed to start and develop any type of relationship with other people or entities.

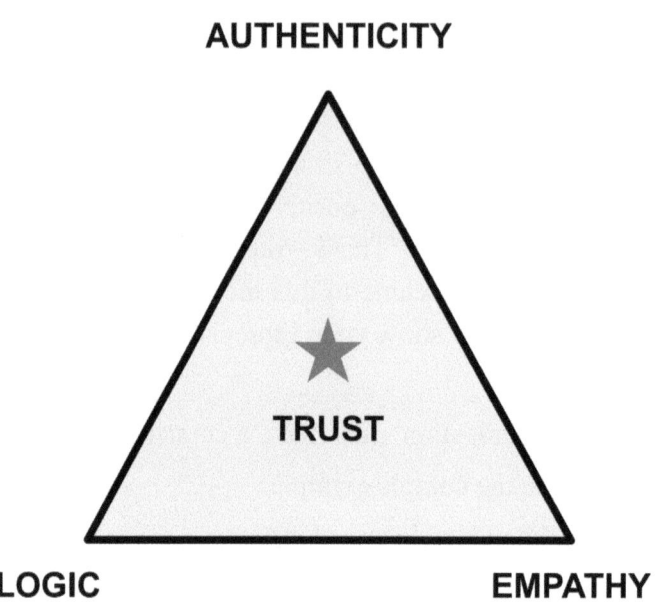

Finally, to summarize this fundamental part of leadership (trust), we can say that there are three simple ways to get more people to trust you: authenticity, logic and empathy.

*Authenticity - Don't pretend to be someone you are not*
Being yourself can be a challenge when you're not surrounded by people who look like you.

When this happens, those who defend the status quo are often rewarded by those who offer a unique perspective.

If we don't show ourselves as we are and if we hide who we are, we are less likely to be trusted. Why? It's because we, as human beings, have the ability to be able to sense in an instant, yes, literally in an instant, if someone is being authentic with us.

And if we can't be trusted to work, you'll be less likely to offer to promote us.

Pay less attention to what you think people want to know about you and much more to what you have to say.

### *Empathy - Connecting with people*

Only those who possess emotional intelligence and are able to perceive and tap into the emotions of the other person or group to guide them to a positive outcome can be effective leaders. Giving others your undivided attention is an important part of empathy.

Empathy is the ability to experience the other person's subjective reality without being affected by it and without losing the perspective of one's own frame. Listen actively, pay attention to the emotional content of what is being explained. Analyze the other party's perception, try to find out how the other party sees the situation. Pay attention to all the communication that is offered to you, both verbal and non-verbal, this will provide you with additional information that will allow you to understand much better what the other party is feeling.

### *Logical - Be logical and consistent*

Many studies state that what defines a leader is not so much his or her philosophy or leadership style as his or her internal "logic of action", i.e. the way he or she interprets his or her environment and reacts when his or her security, confidence or power is challenged. The leader must try to understand his or her own logic of action and ask whether or not it needs to be changed. The leader who chooses to do a self-study of his or her own understanding and development can transform, in addition to his or her own abilities, those of his or her team.

## 2. The charisma and magnetism of the leader

- The three elements of charisma
- False Myths about Charisma
- How to increase your charisma?
- Types of charisma

> *"The reason we were successful, honey?*
> *My overall charisma, of course."*
> Freddy Mercury

What do you think they have in common: Richard Branson, Steve Jobs, Barack Obama, Bob Dylan, James Dean, Mother Teresa of Calcutta, Aung San Suu Kyi, the Dalai Lama, John Lennon and Martin Luther King? There is no doubt that they all exude a certain magnetism. This is what we call charisma.

The Greeks believed that charisma was an offering that the gods gave only to a few. This belief remained and lasted for a very long time. They spoke of it as a magical quality that came with our genetic package. Either you had it or you would never have it. But science has shown that the Greeks were wrong, charisma is built through a series of learned behaviors. In other words, we can learn and develop our charisma.

What is not charisma? We understand that charisma is not something that is already innate, that seems to be linked to beauty, intelligence or the destiny of a few privileged people and that is permanent.

*Leadership: the positive influence*

One of the sociologists par excellence, the German Max Weber, rightly defined charisma as "a certain quality of the individual personality, by virtue of which he is separated from ordinary men and regarded as having powers of supernatural, superhuman or at least extraordinarily exceptional qualities".

In general, a charismatic person is identified by the fact that he or she has:
- style,
- personality,
- visibility,
- confidence,
- success.

But, without a doubt, there is something else about them, something indefinable that makes some people attractive and magnetic because they have the ability to influence others in a positive way by connecting with them physically, intellectually and emotionally.

To be charismatic is to be more inspiring, more persuasive and more influential.

One of the virtues of charismatic people is that they can make others feel special by using very concrete behaviors.

Nobody is born charismatic; charisma is practiced and charisma is learned.

## *THE THREE ELEMENTS OF CHARISMA*

Charisma depends on three elements: presence, power and human warmth.

Presence is the first fundamental element, since people notice when we are attentive, just as they notice when we are absent and inattentive, since through our bodies and involuntarily, we transmit it.

This lack of attention in the conversation can make the other person feel affected and perceive us as insincere people, so that later it will result in a lack of trust, loyalty and relationship with other interlocutors. If this happens, if people perceive us as someone who creates distrust, it will be almost impossible for us to be charismatic.

To be present means to be aware of what is happening at each moment, to pay attention to what is happening, to a concrete fact, instead of being only aware of our own thoughts. It is not easy to be fully present because:

- Our brains are programmed to pay attention to new stimuli, so we are easily distracted, any stimulus tries to capture our attention.
- The constant supply of stimuli can lead us to a state of continuous partial attention, so that we are always partially distracted.

To be present, there are a number of techniques that are very useful and can help you:

- Be physically comfortable: if you don't like your clothes, if you're tired, if you feel overwhelmed by the heat etc. you won't be comfortable. You should try to feel comfortable where you are going, otherwise it will be harder to pay 100% attention to the conversation.

- Be in the here and now: if you have problems that do not belong to the situation you are in at that moment, you may find that when others are explaining things to you and talking to you, you are not thinking about them, but about your personal problem. This will hurt you. You need to be focused on what you are going to do, on the conversation you are having.
- Turn off the cell phone: new technologies have made us addicted to them to the point of needless use. When you want to focus on a specific aspect, leave aside anything that is a distraction, especially the phone.
- The look: this aspect is fundamental, because the look always says everything, the look breathes sincerity. If you look at the other person's eyes, they will feel more confident because they will perceive that you are doing it with your heart.
- Active listening: your body is a clear reflection of your listening. When we are aware of something, such as a conversation, the way we react defines the type of listening we are doing.
- Clarifying questions: asking questions about the topic at hand to clarify concepts shows our presence and attention to the information we are receiving.
- Avoid unnecessary gestures: overreaction generates uncertainty and weirdness, effects that do not help to understand that you are present.
- Waiting: the answers we give must be thoughtful, waiting a few seconds before answering suggests that we are interested and that we have paid attention to what has been transmitted to us.

- A small increase in our ability to be present can have a significant effect on those around us. If we can manage to have a few moments of full presence from time to time, we will make great progress and have a great effect.

Since this is difficult to achieve, we need to find some tips and exercises to practice to improve our presence and get our attention, such as:

- Sounds: look for a sound and concentrate on it, discover through its vibrations where it comes from and its particularities.
- Breathing: identify the rhythm of the breath, the places where the air we breathe passes, how we expel it. Pay attention to the sensations that it provokes and that we are able to perceive.
- Feet: try to focus all your attention on your own feet, more precisely on your toes. If we succeed, we will notice all the physical sensations that run through our body at the same time.
- Eye color: look at the other person and identify the particularity of their eyes, the tone, the hue etc.

In this way, we will be able to focus on a very specific element, so if we practice it in different situations, we will acquire a more focused and concrete ability to concentrate. And over time, we will be able to pay attention to what we are told, avoiding distractions. We can do this because presence is a skill that can be learned, it is a skill that requires practice and patience.

Power is understood as the ability to affect the world around us and to influence others, whether through financial, intellectual, social or physical means. From this definition, we can infer that we see others as powerful because they are able to influence the world around us. This is why people look for clues to an individual's power in their appearance, in their body language, and in the way others react to them.

Every leader must, in some way, be powerful, but it is not as simple as it seems. Achieving power is a slow process that needs to be worked on, and once it is achieved, it needs to be maintained. Here are some techniques that can help us achieve this:

- Increase self-confidence: it is essential to feel that we have power, if we don't believe we have it, who will? We must trust what we think, say and do, we must have more confidence in ourselves.
- To know a little bit about everything. We must be aware of the facts that happen, they can affect us, we must also know the past, so as not to fall into the mistakes already made by others. Being informed and knowing a little bit about everything that surrounds and affects us is essential if we want to be a leader and have power.
- To be physically healthy. If we are not comfortable and healthy, others may not take us seriously. Every person who has power gives an image of themselves and what they stand for.
- Speak slowly and calmly. It is essential to know how to measure the words and expressions we say, every powerful person is clear and concise. We don't want to cause misunderstandings or distort what we say, that's why we have to express ourselves, speak loudly, clearly and slowly.

In short, power could be defined by three concepts: aesthetics, the reactions of others and non-verbal language.

Human warmth is the willingness shown towards others. This quality shows us whether this person will want to use their power for us or against us. This closeness is measured more directly than power, preferably through body language and behavior.

We could say that warmth is a combination of benevolence, altruism and a willingness to make a positive impact on our world towards other beings. All of these qualities are almost impossible to simulate, so it is very difficult to fake warmth.

Before intervening with others, we must be confident and sure of ourselves, if we do not believe we have warmth, we will not have it; if, on the contrary, we believe we have it, we will go far. For this, we can do different exercises in which we identify some positive aspects that we have or things that have happened to us and we think about how to transmit them to others.

In order to achieve this warmth more frequently and with greater ease in front of an audience, there are a series of techniques that can be implemented little by little in practice:

- Be honest in your compliments. It is not necessary that in order for others to be on our side, we promise very good things that we do not know if we can achieve or not. What really matters is to get what we say, to keep our word and to always speak sincerely.

- Work on the warmth of the voice. Everyone can become warm, and one aspect we must control is our voice. We determine it, and we choose how to use it. So, we must seek to control it and manipulate it according to what we need in each moment.

- Copy the other person's non-verbal language. If you want the other person to feel comfortable with you, use gestures similar to theirs. Non-verbal language will help you communicate and connect with the other person.

- Relax your position. It is not necessary to think that there is only one right decision, we need to look at what position we are in and understand the position of others, these can vary, they do not have to be fixed, in fact they should not be.
- Smile and shake hands. Offering warmth to others means offering safety and closeness, talking to people as equals and being safe and friendly, smiling and putting others at ease.
- Anticipate needs and ask for help. We don't always know or have everything we need, asking for help is good, let's be honest. Asking for help makes us brave, we need to make people understand that we all need each other, that exposing our needs does not make us inferior.

Power and warmth are closely related, for someone who is powerful but not warm may impress us, but we will not necessarily perceive him or her as charismatic: he or she may seem cold, arrogant, or distant; someone who possesses warmth without power may be pleasant, but we will not necessarily consider him or her charismatic because he or she may seem too eager to please or desperate to be liked. The two must be linked because they are both necessary conditions for charisma.

Any leader who increases his projection of power, warmth and presence will increase his level of charisma, and if he succeeds in doing so together, he will maximize his potential in an optimal way.

Charisma can be very helpful in developing effective leadership although there are certain costs involved depending on the type of charisma one wants to exercise. Effective leaders must understand the type of charisma they have and the drawbacks associated with it.

The good leader must encourage their natural type of charisma and develop alternative forms.

### *False myths about charisma.*
- Charisma is not just for extroverted and attractive people. Being an introvert can be a great advantage for some charismatic types. They don't feel pressure to be in the spotlight and this allows them to develop certain techniques for being charismatic. Many charismatic people find themselves to be introverts. In Western society, so much attention is paid to the skills and abilities of the extrovert that introverts can end up feeling inferior when in fact several studies show that this is not the case.
- To be charismatic, you have to be attractive. It is true that a good presence is certainly an advantage, but it is not a necessary condition. In fact, charisma makes people more attractive.

What makes a person charismatic? Presence is one of the basic components of charisma. One of the most common ways to describe an individual's charisma is to attribute an "extraordinary presence" to him or her. This is what happens, for example, with Bill Clinton or the Dalai Lama.

### *How to increase your charisma?*
There are ways to increase your "personal magnetism" and the fastest way is the body language method. It is about:

- First, breathe. You can't force anything if you can't regulate your breathing. Think about how you are breathing now. If it is shallow, you are triggering a stress response. It's hard to feel calm, relaxed and confident when you don't have much oxygen and your body thinks it's in attack or flight mode. Make sure you can breathe properly. Avoid tight clothing, for example. Breathe deeply, slowly etc. Full breathing can instantly reduce your stress level, increase your sense of safety and well-being, and even boost your immune system. Take the test. Breathe in slowly to the count of 5, hold your breath for 2 seconds and breathe out again to the count of 5.
- Second, stand up and move your body. Shake your arms and legs. Swing them up and down. Find your balance and place your feet firmly on the floor. A stable and secure posture will help you feel and project more confidence. The primary function of your mind is to monitor your safety, whether it's your ability to escape predators or your ability to stay upright.
- Now imagine you are a big gorilla. Blow up your chest like you want to double your size. Assume that a strong, confident stance will give you more confidence and power. People who adopt expansive postures experience a real physiological change. In a real-world experiment, these positions were found to increase hormones that give confidence and energy by 19% and reduce anxiety hormones by 25%.

If confidence increases, body language acts accordingly. It becomes a biochemical stimulus and the cycle builds on itself. Practice body language based on confidence and it will become second nature to you.

## *Types of charisma.*

There are four types of charisma in business: the focused, the visionary, the gentle and the authoritative.

- Focus: the main focus is on the perception of presence. This attitude gives people the feeling that you are totally with them, listening to them and absorbing what they are saying. This type of charismatic leader makes individuals feel heard and understood. Do not underestimate this type of charisma. It can be very powerful. Elon Musk is an example of this type of charisma.

- The visionary: the visionary inspires others. It makes people believe in something. It can be very effective, but that doesn't mean it convinces others. This is the case with Steve Jobs. He was feared in his company and had many detractors inside and outside the company, but even they admitted that he was a visionary and charismatic.

- The kind person: the charisma of kindness is based on warmth. It connects with the hearts of people and makes them feel welcomed and totally accepted. Mother Teresa of Calcutta is known for this quality.

- Authoritarian: authoritarian charisma is based on the perception of power and the belief that this person has the power to influence our world. This form of charisma is surely the most powerful of all. Our instinctive deference to authority can take on epic proportions and, of course, be entirely positive or negative. Margaret Thatcher is an example of this type of charisma, which is why she is called the "Iron Lady".

*"Charisma has nothing to do with energy, it comes from a clear WHY. It comes from an absolute conviction in an ideal higher than oneself."*
Simon Sinek

## 3. Physical and mental preparation

- Mindset: be prepared to be a leader.
- Physical status: routines.
- Willingness: wanting to be a leader.

> *"I will prepare myself, and one day my chance will come."*
> Abraham Lincoln

At this point, let's talk about the physical and mental preparation of the leader. It is important to specify that leadership is not only an intellectual activity but also a physical activity that requires a great amount of energy and that is why it requires a great physical and mental preparation. In general, leaders maintain a very healthy lifestyle, that is:

- sleep well,
- eat healthy,
- practice releasing tension,
- and have good personal relationships away from toxic people who will consume a lot of our energy.

The pace of life of leaders requires that more and more of them are forced to lead a more orderly life as far as habits are concerned, because wear and tear is important and if one is not and does not stay in good physical and mental condition, it is difficult to become a good leader.

Some examples:

### Bill Gates

The Microsoft founder says he does the dishes every night after dinner with his family, admits it's something he enjoys and despite having other volunteers to do the task, he likes the way he does it.

### Steve Jobs

The founder of Apple, in a 2005 speech at Stanford University, said that every morning he looked in the mirror and asked himself each day if he liked doing what he was supposed to do that day. If for several days the answer was no, he knew he had to change something.

### Mark Zuckerberg

The founder and CEO of Facebook, has been setting himself a different challenge every year for some time now. For example, he learned Mandarin Chinese, traveled all over the United States and only ate meat from animals he hunted himself. In the year that Facebook had scandal after scandal, in 2018, he decided to focus entirely on solving his network.

### Warren Buffet

"I sit in my office and read all day" is what the world's most famous investor said when asked about his daily life in an interview. He estimates that he invests 80% of his time in reading, at the beginning of his career he claimed to read between 600 and 1000 pages a day.

Companies and organizations around the world are investing huge amounts of money to learn more about leadership development. Yet, several research studies and capital analysis certify that 75% of organizations surveyed rated their leadership development programs as ineffective. So, what's going on? Why aren't companies getting more out of their investment in leadership development? Why aren't programs working if you're investing so much in leadership? It's probably because most leadership development courses don't stop at such simple, fundamental aspects of being a good leader and refer to how leaders think: how leaders think, how leaders learn, and how leaders behave.

> *"Luck only favors the well-prepared."*
> Louis Pasteur

There are two examples to illustrate this, one is that of a political leader who isolates himself, perhaps with his family or with his collaborators, in the famous "green room" to prepare himself before a public event and to work on the speech he is going to give and especially to prepare this state of mind of *"I am a leader, I am going to influence, I am going to do it well"*. Similarly, with the example of a rock star, before going on stage, he locks himself in the dressing room, maybe meets with his closest collaborators or partner and prepares for that leadership state. This isolation is applicable to different scenarios.

It is the leaders mind that will guide them as to what information they will use to deal with the situations they will face. So, it's easy, the leader's mind is the one that decides to push and the one that decides why.

In a common example, two different leaders may be faced with the same situation (e.g., a disagreement with one of their co-workers) and handle and respond to that situation in very different ways. While one leader might see the situation as a threat to his or her authority, another might see it as an opportunity to learn and grow further.

If the investment a company or professional makes in leadership development ignores mindset and thinking, it in turn ignores how leaders see, perceive, and interpret problems and opportunities of this type.

And at this point, if mindsets are so important, what kind of mindset should help their leaders develop? There is social science research that will help us understand the different mindsets that individuals may have. In it, we identify four different types of behaviors that have been found to influence leaders' ability to interact with others, better manage change, and more effectively fulfill their roles as leaders.

- Growth and fixed mindsets. A growth mindset is the complete confidence that all people, including oneself, can change and develop their abilities, skills and intelligence. In contrast, a fixed mindset does not believe that people can change their abilities, skills and intelligence.

- After decades of research in this area, it has been determined that people with a growth mindset are mentally prepared to meet and take on new challenges, adopt and adapt the most effective problem-solving strategies, take advantage of developmental feedback to their subordinates, and demonstrate perseverance in the pursuit of goals.

- Learning and performance mindsets. A learning mindset requires constant motivation to increase one's skills and master something new. This type of mindset focuses on getting favorable judgments (or avoiding negative judgments) about one's skills. Leaders with this type of learning mindset, compared to those with a performance mindset, are better prepared to increase their skills, engage in deep learning strategies, and put in more effort. They are also persistent, adaptable, willing to cooperate, and tend to act at a higher level.

- Deliberative and implementation mindsets. Leaders with a deliberative mindset have a greater capacity to receive all kinds of information to ensure that they think and act in the most optimal way. Implementation-minded leaders are more focused on making decisions, sometimes in a hurry, which closes them off to new and different ideas and information. Deliberative-minded leaders tend to make better decisions because they are more impartial, more accurate, and less biased in their processing and decision making.

- Promotional and preventive mindsets. Promotional minded leaders focus on winning and gaining, that is their main objective. They set a specific challenge, goal or objective and prioritize making progress. In contrast, prevention-minded leaders focus on avoiding losses and anticipating problems at all costs. Promotive leaders are more likely to think positively, more open to change, more diligent in persevering through challenges and setbacks, and demonstrate a higher level of role development and innovative behaviors than preventive leaders.

When we understand these mindsets, we can tailor our leadership training programs to locate the most effective employees.

As leaders are able to define, self-assess and cultivate each other, their thinking, learning and behavior will naturally improve because they will see and interpret their situations more effectively.

### *Physical fitness: routines*

Certain factors can prevent the mental state of the leader from being adequate to project charisma, obstacles to presence, power and warmth, we speak of physical and mental discomfort.

- Physical discomfort: any discomfort that affects our external state, what others can see of us, influences people's perception of our ability to influence others. To avoid this, we must:
  - Prevent: prevent the discomfort from occurring and developing.
  - Acknowledge and remain vigilant. Let's be aware of where we are and how we feel at any given time and, if we are not well, let's fix it.

- Act and remedy: explain why we are going in a certain direction or behaving in a certain way.

- Mental discomfort: although it originates in the mind, it can affect the rest of the body and therefore the way people see us. It can be the result of different problems of internal negativity that we have had and they can be an obstacle for the development of personal charisma. These problems are usually the following:
    - Anxiety: caused by uncertainty. Not knowing what will happen, how, when etc. can produce anxiety because we are not able to bear the uncertainty that some situations imply. This can be an obstacle at the moment of negotiation and a great disadvantage for charisma because it affects our internal state making it difficult to be present on the spot and decreasing confidence and the ability to transmit warmth.

        To alleviate this discomfort, we can practice different techniques such as the transfer of responsibility, which helps us to feel less affected, close our eyes, breathe deeply several times imagining the air going in and out perceiving how we expel with it all the worries and concerns, think of someone who always helps us and finally get rid of everything seeing the different sensations.

    - Dissatisfaction: due to comparisons. People tend to compare their experiences, especially when they have several options to choose from and want to make the best decision. By trying to optimize the outcome, we interfere with our presence, which makes us nervous and dissatisfied. To avoid this tendency, the technique of shifting responsibility can also be used.

- Self-criticism. The way we see and feel about ourselves has a great impact on how we act. When we criticize ourselves, our mind perceives it as an attack, which influences our reactions and the way others perceive us.

    You doubt me. The confidence we have or don't have in our own ability to achieve something has a great influence on how we express ourselves and how we are perceived. We need to know that these doubts we have about ourselves are increased when we are at great risk.

If we are able to identify both types of discomfort and find the solution, we will address them and become charismatic leaders with greater ease and security.

To be a leader, you have to want to be one. The desire to be a leader has even led some people to transform themselves physically, to train, to learn new disciplines and to develop leadership skills and abilities. Let's remember the statement we have been commenting on since the beginning of this book, the leader is not born a leader but made a leader, so if someone wants to become a leader, he has to train in the field to achieve it and this training is not only mental but also physical.

## 4. Create your own brand

- What is your brand?
- How to build your own brand?
- The attitude

*"When I was a child, my mother told me: 'If you become a soldier, you will be a general. If you are a monk you will end up as a Pope. I chose to be a painter, and I became Picasso."*
Pablo PICASSO

The concept of personal brand is on the agenda and yet it seems that not everyone has understood that he/she is a brand. This famous personal brand is fundamental for the leader, regardless of his/her industry or country.

"I will follow you etc. I will buy you". Your name, your personal brand or personal branding, refers to one of the most current marketing trends. Using our personal brand is the most valuable resource every leader has and with it you must learn to differentiate yourself from others.

The presence of digital tools will help make this concept work by increasing the power in you, helping you in your positioning.

And why work on your personal brand? Mainly because people prefer to talk to people rather than brands, they want to hear from a person in their industry and not a "company" with no name.

*Leadership: the positive influence*

By positioning your company, you position yourself as an expert and this will allow you to reach a larger number of potential customers, all your know-how will be transferred to your company.

Your personal brand will generate trust in your professional relationships, in your projects and in your sales, you will have more opportunities to reach a wider audience than perhaps as a commercial brand or as a company.

And of course, it will improve your own personal satisfaction.

If you develop your personal brand properly, you will gain admiration and good reputation in your industry.

To achieve your goal, you must differentiate yourself. You have talents and skills that, combined with your experience, provide value to your knowledge.

> *"Be yourself, all other personalities are already taken."*
> Oscar Wilde

Send a clear message: what you are offering and to whom you are offering it. You must identify your audience and be specific in your explanations. Your potential customers need to understand exactly what benefit they get from you if you are the one.

Remember, with your personal brand, you are a business. When you present yourself with confidence, you show why you are different from others, which helps you get better results and encourages others to talk about you.

You need to create an emotional connection. People make many decisions based on their emotions and feelings, and people will remember how you made them feel. In that sense, two basic points:

1. Speak and communicate with your audience. Search for your contacts, interlocutors and potential customers (internal or external). Find out where they are and share your opinions and experiences with them. Learn to listen to the needs and goals of your stakeholders.
2. Connect and expand your audience. Take advantage of the benefits and accessibility that the internet offers, let your contacts connect you. Take care of your social networks, update your profiles, invest time in creating conversations inside and outside the internet, this will allow you to build long term relationships. You will be able to create a phrase that identifies you so that others will remember you.

In a simple way, we can define personal branding as a way to share our good name, experiences, successes, desires and identity in a solid and firm way. A personal brand is built around oneself, which usually means that the brand name is associated with the personal name.

It is a powerful resource for any professional that can generate great opportunities. The personal brand is the digital footprint of that person, it is their DNA. It's not only his or her style, experience or knowledge, but also the way we transmit them, our values and how we make others feel.

Cultivating the personal brand allows you to ensure that your audience sees you as you want them to see you, and by extension, your business.

In short, those determined to use their personal brand to amplify the value of their work or professional collaboration must build, promote, communicate and protect it. This is just as important, if not more so, than the project itself.

Make your mark! It doesn't matter if you work in your own company, in a public entity or in a multinational! Any professional can create their own brand. Leaders should certainly have one etc. Aren't Bill Gates, Steve Jobs and Mark Zuckerberg a brand themselves?

### *PERSONAL BRAND LEADERS*

To start building our personal brand, we must not be lazy in knowing ourselves, because this self-knowledge is about our strengths and weaknesses, our attitudes and skills, but also our preferences, needs, desires, limiting beliefs, etc. - our identity in the end - is what will allow us to define the goals we want to achieve and to develop strategies.

Therefore, it is obvious that the positioning of oneself in the job market is important, although the personal brand is always observed as a broader concept. There is no doubt that there must be consistency in all facets of your life, as there must be between your analog and digital world. We can't be completely different people in one environment or the other, or we won't be credible and we won't get hired.

Our actions are samples of our personality, our values and our culture. Imagine how important this is for a leader, who has to cooperate with his team and partners not only to achieve results but also to do so with a good disposition, with added value, maintaining a high degree of motivation and well-being among his interlocutors.

These are the qualities that make the leader act like a leader-coach, that he is the best in his role, that he will be remembered when he is gone. We will undoubtedly be seduced by the security he conveys in himself and in his potential. However, it is better for leaders to add the value of their brand to the company and its professional network, which will enrich and broaden the strategic possibilities.

The most interesting leaders are the ones I can learn more about by reading their blog, attending one of their conferences, or discovering their opinions in the forums; all of which will help me build a fairly accurate picture of someone I want to be able to encourage to continually engage and evolve, as well as inspire enthusiastic attitudes towards the common project that is the company.

A leader is indeed someone to inspire, someone whose credibility is beyond doubt, someone to emulate in some way. All this generates commitment, trust and a spirit of collaboration.

Here are the 5 key elements you need to develop this important strategy, your personal brand:

### 1. *Passion*

That attitude that spreads the energy and that you convey when you speak or present your business plan is what will create the halo of magic towards your idea. Passion is more important than the business plan itself and its compensation package. Without passion you will not convince anyone.

Your enthusiasm will be the trigger to generate more buy-in. Passion is a powerful key to closing a deal, sometimes even more than logic.

### 2. Positive attitude

Antoine Saint-Exupéry's well-known phrase, *"The meaning of things is not in the things themselves, but in our attitude toward them"*, makes sense at this point. Your attitude is one of the ingredients you will need to develop your personal growth. It is the attitude we have towards life and towards our project or business that will determine our success. People like to be around others who have positive feelings and actions that they can relate to.

You can do this little test:

Make a decision to have positive thoughts, phrases and comments for a period of 4 hours while you are working. Try to be as conscious as possible of every word or thought you have and avoid making negative statements or references. When you have completed the test, ask yourself if you liked the results and if you know what to do with the rest of your life.

### 3. Contribution

Your personal brand will be closely tied to the contribution you can generate in the marketplace. If you provide relevant information and solutions, you will contribute to a much stronger brand.

## 4. Know your product, your service, your company

It is a priority and very important for any leader to have the right answers about their business. Keep in mind the list of benefits and try to memorize them or be able to access this checklist at any time. Having knowledge of all the critical points and knowing how to guide your prospects to develop improvements on your concept product is the key to your own success.

## 5. Marketing

The tools you use to promote your brand and the skills you demonstrate to express your ideas, vision and business concept will be fundamental. There are no shortcuts here. You have to work and take on the responsibility that comes with being a leader in an industry. This marketing process requires a thorough understanding of all the tools and an initial assessment of which one will best support your personal branding strategy.

> *"Do not imitate anything or anyone. A lion that copies a lion becomes a monkey."*
> Victor Hugo

# CHAPTER III

# THE LEADERS
# AND THE OTHERS

*Leadership: the positive influence*

# THE LEADER AND THE OTHERS

## 1. The leader's environment

- What is the environment: things, people, other leaders, etc.
- How to identify it: STAKEHOLDERS MAP, the great living tool.
- How to extend it: the creation of networks and alliances: how to create and enrich networks

> *"I must follow the people, Am I not their leader?"*
> Benjamin Disraeli

In this chapter, we will deal with the leader's environment and those who constitute it: how to identify his stakeholders, how to create and enrich his network.

Being a leader today means assuming and accepting that in order to fulfill your commitments, you need the support of others; it is not enough to have a vision, you need followers to be a leader. The figure of the lone hero who single-handedly transformed organizations is misplaced.

Today, leadership means recognizing the importance of relationships to succeed in the changing reality of business. And when is this changing reality of organizations most evident? There is no reality more changeable than that which emerges in a crisis environment.

Today, leadership operates in a complex, uncertain organizational context and in interaction not only with the Covid crisis but with all other ongoing transformations. Due to the challenges that organizations are facing, it is necessary to reduce complexity and uncertainty in order to obtain a more desirable picture of the future. This is why leaders must have a strong sense of purpose and a clear vision. And this vision must be shared by the members of the organization.

The leader must involve his or her people in the organizational change process. Not all members will participate with the same intensity, but the leader must get them involved. He will consult with his closest colleagues and ask them for proposals to be discussed at the appropriate organizational levels.

A leader must be able to create, design and anticipate new organizational scenarios that will lead to success by anticipating events. Successful companies are constantly looking for people who can lead.

Some experts believe that the key to success lies in the creative activity of creating new paths, not in imitating and/or following existing ones. The idea then arises to consider changing the paradigm that long-term success comes from stability, consistency, harmony, discipline and consensus. On the other hand, being conservative can lead to failure.

## Who are the stakeholders?

This concept, created in the 1980s by American philosopher Robert Edward Freeman and frequently used in leadership, defines a stakeholder as any individual or organization that is in some way influenced by the actions of a certain company.

Mr. Freeman argued that stakeholders are fundamental, indispensable and should always be considered in the strategic planning of any project or enterprise.

In this way, understand that the success or failure of any business will always affect not only its owners but also everyone around it, i.e. its employees, its partners, its suppliers, its competitors, the families of all the people involved and of course, its customers.

## What is the impact of stakeholders on a company?

As mentioned earlier, stakeholders refer to a group of people who are affected by a company's decisions.

However, the reverse is also true. The satisfaction of these people or organizations will also have a strong influence on the results and objectives set by the companies.

That's why it's important to ensure that all of your company's stakeholders are satisfied with the work you do. From your customers to your shareholders, they all have a great value for your company and their wishes and demands will have a direct impact on your organization's results.

The great mission of leaders of companies with a wide variety of stakeholders is precisely to find common goals among all the individuals and organizations involved in their business. Only in this way is it possible to foster sustainable growth for your organization.

Therefore, the importance of stakeholders in your company is very high. In addition to all this, it is necessary to align the objectives and expectations of all those who are part of this group in order for your actions and projects to achieve the expected success.

How can your company succeed if, for example, customers, who are also stakeholders, are no longer interested in your product or service, and if your company's employees are no longer as motivated and cannot achieve a certain level of productivity?

If your company generates little value, the impact on shareholders, investors and banks, for example, will also be very significant. In other words, all of your company's stakeholders are linked to each other and the lack of satisfaction of one group has a direct effect on the behaviour of another.

That's why it's essential to broaden the vision of the group of stakeholders interested in your company's actions so that you can understand what they are looking for and set common goals to guide your organization in a sustainable and effective way.

### *What are the types of stakeholders and how do you manage them?*

Primary stakeholders are all those who are essential to the normal operation and development of the company.

In this way, we want to re-emphasize the idea that it is all the people who have a direct economic link with the company and that this is where shareholders, partners, employees and customers come in.

Secondary stakeholders are those who are not directly involved in the business, but who, while not primary, will also be affected by the business's results. This includes competitors, the market or people in general.

## *What is networking?*

Networking is the concept that basically refers to establishing and strengthening relationships with other people who share our interests or profession. That is, what we have done all our lives when we went for a coffee with people from our social or professional environment, and who says coffee, says lunch or dinner, goes to events, etc.

The writer who goes to the book fair in his town is creating a network, the fan who goes to the comic book festival where he can meet this or that actor or cartoonist, or spend time chatting with others like him, is also creating a network, and so we could go on with many other examples.

Networking should be considered as it is something very useful to get to know each other, to listen and learn from others' experiences, or to find new opportunities and, who knows, it is also a good place to make new friends.

Without a doubt, networking can also be helpful in strengthening your leadership. You won't get it all done by leading your team from your chair on the other side of your desk.

## *Who can I network with and what can they do for me?*

- **People in your immediate environment**

    Very often we think about networking from the outside, but we don't think about building good relationships with our colleagues and the customers and suppliers we work with on a daily basis.

- **People who are outside your environment.**

    There are people outside of this environment, closer to you but beyond the work environment or your closest personal circle.

    We should not underestimate the value of relationships outside our environment, especially since they are a huge source of experience and knowledge. We all learn things from listening to other people, other experts or even from talking to someone who was a stranger to you before.

    Of course, it is also very useful to establish relationships with other companies, agencies and institutions. Some may represent the same or very similar functions to yours, and others may be completely unrelated.

    You never know if, in the future, you might need the help of that person to whom no one spends a few minutes, inviting her to coffee and taking an interest in what she was doing, thanking her for her time and offering a smile.

- **Your superiors, your managers, your board.**

    We need to network with our hierarchy, although it should be noted that this should not be the primary focus of our efforts in this regard. Unless you are thinking only of yourself and seeking only short-term visibility, you should strive to cultivate more beneficial long-term relationships, such as with subordinates, colleagues, or people outside your environment.

If you have been working effectively at the top of your team, and your team has been developing well, handling difficult situations, your work, other people, and especially your subordinates, will make much of your networking easier in front of your superiors. This doesn't mean that you don't occasionally talk to your immediate boss (if you have one), because he or she, among others, is your supervisor and will give you instructions and direction for your work. It is normal that if you have achieved results, if you are an honest and sincere person, and if you have behaved like a good leader, this will change and the relationship with your boss will become closer and friendlier.

- **The bosses of our bosses.**

    Sooner or later, the opportunity will arise to meet with the owners of the company, perhaps even the top of the organization or company to which you belong.

    It's a good thing you're taking advantage of this unique opportunity. Even if, in most cases, you don't know that you've made a great and genuine impression on this important position.

    Try to do your job as well as possible. Strive to help those who have fewer opportunities than you to be known and successful. In any case, even if the person at the top of the power structure is not able to appreciate the leader you are, be sure that you will have done a thorough job on your staff. It would be a bit like indirectly networking on them.

- **People who hold similar positions to ours.**

    It can also be very interesting to get in touch with other people who are doing similar work or in similar positions, as they can bring their experience to you.

    This is a good way to introduce yourself to your respective areas of influence and to get to know your staff.

    If that person is a good leader, and has earned the loyalty and respect of his or her team, getting his or her approval can be a determining factor in how you relate to his or her team members, even if it seems silly.

    Also, maybe tomorrow you will take over as leader of that team, or maybe you will get a promotion and these people will become your closest associates. Think that if you have built relationships with them in the past, and have been able to earn their respect as a teammate, it will be much easier for you to be recognized as a leader.

- **Media**

    In some cases of political or business leadership, it may also be important to know the journalists and media.

    The famous 4th power as Edmund Burke said in 1787.

    Undoubtedly, we can include in this category the social networks that play a fundamental role in the information field.

- **Even competitors (or colleagues from other companies)**

    We can also establish relationships with colleagues working in other companies.

- **Last but not least,** the foundation of any business is our people.

This is perhaps one of the least appreciated forms of networking by those who seek success at all costs without properly valuing the work of their collaborators, nor having the intention of helping them improve and progress, among other things for fear of being overshadowed.

These individuals will never be able to coach their own team beyond the requirements of their salary.

The relationships with your employees will be a great source of inspiration and invaluable to your leaders.

Your interest in dealing with the entire staff and how you do it is probably one of the most important factors in developing your leadership.

This is where you will gain the respect of those who will follow you when the critical moments come. The road is long, although in reality it has no secrets, it is not difficult.

But, and this is how we end this chapter, beware etc. it's not about networking with a win-win mentality or getting something in return. That would be mean and unethical.

Don't worry so much about the benefits you can get from these relationships, you'd better worry about giving value to these people.

If your connections tell others above them about you and your work, if they see you as their true leader and follow you wherever you go, if every person you meet has a good impression of your authentic self, with its virtues and flaws, be clear that the benefits will come.

> *"You can make more friends in two months if you take an interest in others than you can in two years if you wait for others to take an interest in you."*
> Dale Carnegie

## 2. Empathy

- What is it?
- How does it work? Concrete techniques.
- The limits of empathy: being assertive versus being selfish.

> *"Empathy is simply about listening, holding space, being non-judgmental, connecting emotionally, and communicating this incredibly healing message: you are not alone."*
> Brené Brown

At this point, we are going to talk about a fundamental issue in leadership, namely the issue of empathy. According to a UN report on world happiness, Denmark is one of the happiest countries in the world. The data comes from a major survey that has ranked the happiness of 155 countries around the world since 2012. For seven consecutive years, Denmark has been one of the three happiest countries. The fact that since 1993 it has been mandatory to teach empathy in schools has contributed to this country's status.

Empathy helps build relationships, prevent harassment and achieve professional success. It promotes growth in leaders, entrepreneurs and managers. Empathetic people tend to be more successful because they ignore the more narcissistic behaviours of their peers and are only goal-oriented.

Empathy is what makes the difference between two human beings and also between two leaders, one effective and the other not. Traditionally, empathy refers to the capacity we have to put ourselves in the other's shoes, here we will analyze that it is something more complex.

Empathy has been defined as one of the capabilities that form the basis of modern leadership and the more technologized the world becomes, the more companies need to be led by people who are considered emotionally capable.

This importance of empathy is particularly important in crisis situations such as during the Covid epidemic, because social distance can jeopardize the bond, yet empathy remains fundamental.

The ultimate enemy of empathy is ego. The least empathetic are the most egocentric because they just think and talk about it. This can go to more dramatic extremes, such as psychopathy. A psychopath is someone who has no empathy because they don't take into account that they are hurting the other person.

Unbridled or excessive empathy also carries risks, as you can end up serving the other party and you can be the other party's slave. The balance is in the assertiveness. You can be so empathetic that it undermines your interests or goals, so you need to be assertive while respecting the other person.

When someone has the opportunity to work with an empathetic leader, they will not forget and will always remember. The ability to be listened to calmly, to have people take their time and give you their full attention, has a profound impact. In this way, a leader is able to make each person feel unique and at the same time part of a cohesive team.

On the other hand, we find an empathetic employee, if he is more able to create a good network of relationships within the company, which is beneficial both for his own career and for the creation of a positive work environment. In addition, they will be able to handle complex situations and learn from their mistakes.

Empathy is a difficult skill to acquire, it requires a lot of practice and a real personal interest, but there is no doubt that it is the basis of good communication and modern leadership: it allows us to inspire and persuade others, as well as to create quality interpersonal relationships.

### *Enhanced leadership skills*

Showing a genuine interest in the other person's truth is the key to creating quality relationships and connections - taking an interest in the other person, opening up to understand how they see the world, doing your best to try to understand them even if you don't agree with them, understanding their attitudes, feelings, actions, hopes, fears and desires and responding appropriately.

To be empathetic, we need to spend time with people, with team members, with other collaborators, to listen carefully and to dialogue. This can be in meetings or in informal conversations in any meeting place: following the lives of people with whom we have a regular relationship creates very effective working relationships. With empathy, you can really understand the other person and therefore build bridges to create strong relationships and find solutions to possible conflicts.

For a company, establishing and fostering empathetic working relationships is a way to attract and retain talent (and keep employees wanting to work with us), and also, to distinguish itself as a humanized company.

The three key steps that characterize an empathic relationship:

1. Listen and ask questions with a genuine interest and an open mind, without prejudice, to what the other person is saying. Listen silently to everything the other person wants to say without interrupting. Avoid giving advice.
2. By asking ourselves what we did not understand, we should not let ourselves be in doubt. Confirm from time to time what the other has just said, showing that we are paying attention. Try to ask if the perception we received is the one they wanted to give us or also to see the situation together, from different sides.
3. Give a brief summary in conclusion of what was heard to confirm that it was understood. This is also a good time to recognize a skill or quality in the other person.

### *Empathy for customers*

The corporate culture of empathy is paramount in customer relations. In this area, it is more necessary than ever to train employees so that they are able to always consider the customer in everything they do and provide the best possible experience.

To this end, we propose the following recommendations:
- That all the company's staff know the customer well: access to market research, interviews, call center recordings, store visits, complaint sharing, their behavior on social networks etc.
- Provide hands-on training that conveys what is and is not empathic treatment with real-life situations. Redesign of client service protocols based on training.

- Create company habits that give a real presence to the customer: like the "customer chair" in meetings, specific visualization for customers in project development, build empathy cards that allow to know in depth the type of customer etc.

In other words, make empathy one of the key values in decision making. That's how relevant it is.

### *Selfishness versus assertiveness*

Linked to selfishness, the assertive subject presents the right to decide who to help and who not to help. Without falling into ruinous differences. He does not feel obliged by the law, but acts by conviction.

Literal definition of selfishness: excessive self-love that makes one too self-interested.

The egocentric subject thinks "I am the center of the universe" and, inevitably, he leaves the others aside, which is not the case of the assertive subject: he takes care of his own interest without forgetting the others. The assertive subject does not recognize himself better than the other, "I am better than you", but "I am at least equal to you".

*Leadership: the positive influence*

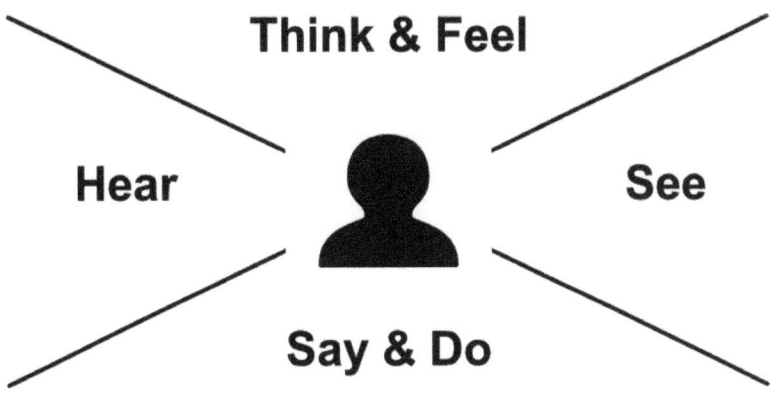

In leadership, to summarize and end on this point, having empathy is what shows that we are not enemies and therefore you can follow me and accompany me because I will not hurt you. There are studies that show that the first question you mentally ask yourself when you meet someone and answer within seconds is whether that person is a friend or foe. Leaders develop empathy because they don't want their followers to see them as an obstacle or an enemy, which would prevent them from following them.

*"If you don't have empathy and effective personal relationships, no matter how smart you are, you won't get very far."*
Daniel Goleman

## 3. Influence

- Influence versus manipulation
- 10 manipulation strategies
- How to exercise influence?
- Techniques to develop it

> *"Leading by example is not the primary way to influence others, it is the only way."*
> Albert Einstein

We move on to two concepts that every leader needs to know very clearly to be able to identify and differentiate them: influence and manipulation, two related but radically opposed concepts. One of the key elements to differentiate them is the concept of "good faith" versus bad faith, a legal concept recognized in most of the world's legal systems: what is your intention? In this sense, manipulation responds to the bad faith of the manipulator, while influence responds to the good faith of taking into account the interests of the other party. Another key element in differentiating them is what happens in the long run; while manipulation jeopardizes the relationship and the long run, influence can strengthen the relationship.

Thus, while it is true that the good leader must try to influence his or her environment to obtain sufficient support to achieve his or her objective, the good leader will avoid at all costs the risk of manipulating others, and the risk of being manipulated.

However, to avoid manipulating and being manipulated, it is essential to know exactly what manipulation is. The dictionary definition is: "the action of directing the behavior of a person, in one's own interest, without the person realizing it and against his or her own interests".

Neither the manipulator nor the manipulated will benefit in the long run from manipulation. It is in the short term that a manipulative strategy can help to achieve certain results. Results by which, in the mind of the manipulator, he will justify the means used. But if this is your way, you should consider substituting other methods of ethical influence that give you respect.

In other words, influence is a win-win proposition. Where manipulation is internally focused, influence is externally focused.

The fundamental element, and fundamental to effective and ethical influence, is trust. Manipulators are heard, but persuaders are believed because they are honest, loyal. If there is no trust, the leader's audience only listens on one level: and what are the consequences? With trust, an audience cares about what is being said and also gives the message the opportunity to mean something at multiple levels, yours and the leader's.

Manipulation is meant to be exposed as such and exudes immediate contempt when this reality is perceived. Those subjected to manipulation may sometimes try to find ways to survive in order to get even, and these goals are hardly consistent with the common goals of the team.

According to Professor Noam Chomsky, there are 10 strategies of manipulation that we will detail below, to try to identify them, to anticipate them and not to fall victim to them:

1. The distraction strategy. This strategy consists of diverting the attention of the interlocutor from important issues by means of the technique of flooding or continuous distractions or unimportant information.
2. Create problems and then propose solutions. This method, called "problem-reaction-solution", consists in creating a problem, so that the manipulated person accepts the actions that allow to solve the problem.
3. The strategy of gradualness. Basically, this technique consists in gradually making acceptable a measure that is unacceptable. When we take a long-term perspective, we see what we have accepted.
4. The difference strategy. A technique also widely used in manipulation is to postpone the implementation of a painful decision. Since the decision has no immediate effects we consider it more acceptable. It is easier to accept a future sacrifice than an immediate one, we have a naive vision that everything will be better tomorrow.
5. Address the audience as little creatures. To manipulate an adult audience, there is nothing better than to address them as if they were children of 12 years or younger with childish language and tone, so that adults unconsciously act and react like children.
6. Use the emotional aspect much more than the reflective one. This is a very classic and well-known technique, the use of

emotions is a classic technique to short-circuit the rational analysis, and finally the critical sense of the individuals.

7. Keeping the public ignorant and mediocre. Keeping people ignorant of the real situation or withholding key information is another technique widely used to manipulate people, either individually or collectively.

8. Encourage the public to be complacent about mediocrity. Encourage the public to believe that it is fashionable to be stupid, vulgar and uneducated.

9. Reinforce self-blame. To make the individual believe that he is the only one responsible for his own misfortune, because of the insufficiency of his intelligence, his capacities or his efforts. In this way, the individual accepts his or her own fate.

10. Knowing individuals better than they know themselves. Thanks to biology, neurobiology and applied psychology, we can have an advanced knowledge of the human being, both physically and psychologically. This allows us to know individuals and groups much better than they know themselves and to act on them with more control and mastery than we imagine.

Winston Churchill used to say that *"influence is not about getting others to do what I want, but about getting them to want to do what I want them to do"*. This phrase perfectly defines the ability to influence the decisions of others.

Few people consider influence to be part of their job. It is mostly attributed to politicians or businessmen with questionable ethics. Nothing could be further from the truth. If influence is positive, responsible and for the common good, it should be part of communication and leadership and every professional should develop it.

Anyone can be persuasive. It is a skill like others we have discussed throughout this book that can be acquired, that can be learned. The secrets of persuasive communication can be learned and applied easily and successfully in a professional environment, regardless of the position held.

### *How to exercise it? Techniques to develop it*

In ancient Rome, it was said that a good leader had *potestas* (power of influence) and a bad *auctoritas* (authority). Authority can be imposed, but influence will always be given. In a professional environment, the ability to persuade will depend on the perception of the environment and the credibility that others give you, not on your position in the company as explained earlier. Persuading is a complex skill that will help you achieve your long-term goals. Before you embark on the task of convincing others, practice the behavioral techniques listed below that will help you strengthen your leadership.

### *Influencing Techniques*

1. **Listen carefully to the person you are talking to**

    It is necessary to listen and ask a number of questions. This requires energy and patience on your part, but it will also be seen as an act of generosity. It is a way to get to know the person you are talking to and to know exactly what solution he or she brings to your problem.

2. **Select the information**

    Behave in a sincere and honest way, even if it does not mean that you tell everything you know. A good leader must choose what information he or she provides to others, how to process it, and how to interpret it. Sometimes you will have to omit data and sometimes you will have to offer irrelevant information that will distract the other person or unconsciously influence them.

3. **Lifting the ego of your interlocutor**

    Don't go too far, but rather focus on the person you are talking to. They should like who they are and feel comfortable in your presence.

4. **Always think positive**

    No one will succeed in persuading another person by using negative phrases or concepts. You should not blame others, criticize their work, or show contempt. Keep words like "impossible" or "failure" out of your vocabulary.

5. **Admit that you made a mistake**

    If you admit your mistakes and failures, the other party will feel confident and open up to you easily. If you admit your mistakes, the other party will admit yours as well. This will increase your credibility.

6. **Don't let doubt creep in**

   Don't use phrases like "maybe", "we'll see" or "I think". Take a clear position and make concrete proposals. Don't leave the other person in doubt.

7. **Be an expert on your subject!**

   You must know your topic thoroughly. You should speak briefly and concisely, but you should be prepared to answer very specific questions.

8. **Hold the excitement**

   Be enthusiastic, don't hesitate to speak from the heart. If you are boring, it will greatly reduce the impact of your speech. On the contrary, if you communicate with enthusiasm and are open, the attention and interest of your interlocutor will be increased. Enthusiasm, empathy, sincerity and honesty are more convincing than the best rational arguments. If you want to persuade someone, appeal to their emotions using your own feelings.

9. **Get straight to the point.**

   When you want to persuade someone, you must be clear and brief in your speech. Don't bore your interlocutor with details that are not important, and remember that your speech must be concise, because the longer it is, the more your interlocutor will get tired of listening to you.

**10. Build a relationship.**

Establish a healthy and sincere relationship with your partner. If possible, spend more time with him/her to understand and know his/her needs. The most important thing is to gain your partner's trust.

> *"Nothing is so contagious as example."*
> La Rochefoucauld

## 4. Communication

- Types of communication
- The rules for achieving positive impact and influence
- The importance of non-verbal language for leadership

> *"The most important thing in communication is to hear what has not been said."*
> Peter Drucker

Communication is a key element for people and for society in general, therefore, it is also a fundamental element of organizations and of the leader. The leader must be able to influence, motivate and guide his team members and followers, and the way to do this is through communication.

Effective communication and effective leadership go hand in hand, we cannot have one without the other. This communication takes all its place in a context like the one generated by the Covid crisis. Our means and techniques of communication have changed, especially with the omnipresence of video conferences. However, the objective of communication remains the same; to connect us with others.

The starting point of communication and leadership is listening. In leadership, we always start by listening rather than talking.

*Leadership: the positive influence*

> *"We have two ears and one mouth to hear twice as much as we speak."*
> Epictet

When you listen, you are already communicating because you are conveying to the other party that you are interested in what they are saying. You show respect with active listening. What you need to do as a leader is to listen to people in order to integrate that vital information that will serve to complete your vision. Then, when you present and communicate it, people will already be convinced of what you are communicating and sharing.

While it is true that all or most of us are aware and think that communication is the most important part of most things, in practice it is the most forgotten part.

Communication is the primary means by which the leader communicates and shares his vision with his environment. It is not enough to have great ideas, a great vision and a solid strategy, you have to be able to communicate them to share them.

Effective leaders are responsible for establishing formal and informal communication networks that will help them accurately guide the knowledge of the people they lead. That's why two of the functions of communication that a good leader must have are: knowing how to listen to their people and knowing how to explain things clearly.

A leader's vision and motivation are meaningless if he or she cannot convey his or her ideas to others. The leader must be able to communicate his ideas and at the same time understand the ideas of others in order to guide them. Communication must be reciprocal: I transmit what I want and I listen to you so that you can transmit to me if you have understood.

Communicating at all times with the team, due to the different situations that arise daily and tend to find solutions, for management decision making is one of the most important skills and abilities that a leader must develop to become an effective leader.

It is one of the fundamental pillars of the proper functioning of any company, organization or business.

Generally speaking, we can see that within the same company, we can clearly differentiate two types of communication:

- External: this is all communication aimed at the organization's external audiences. It is part of corporate communication because its main objective is to transmit and improve the image, reputation and message to be sold. This type of communication is used both to send information to the public and to receive information from those who want to send it.

    A good external communication strategy will make us visible on the market and allow us to compete with our competitors.

- Internal: all communication that takes place between the members of the company within the company. It stems from the need to understand each other and to work together, which increases the good climate in the company. A good internal communication plan will help to create a pleasant and transparent environment.

Good management of internal communication strategy and actions is reflected in the results you get from your team.

As far as our work team is concerned, the communication that must exist between us must be fluid, honest, spontaneous and natural. Forced communication will not be beneficial and will damage the relationship between team members, leading to possible misunderstandings. In the team, we must treat each other with respect and say what we really believe, speaking sincerely, but always without offending.

There are many ways to communicate, and we will not do it in the same way with all colleagues or clients or media. To clients, if it is a big company, we can communicate our new offers or what we want by e-mail, but if we want to make an appointment with another company to negotiate, we can talk to each other by phone, and when we see each other, we will do it face to face or by video conference.

It is important that we keep in mind that when we speak face to face with another person, our voice is not the only instrument that communicates, our body also through its movements, gestures, posture. That is why we should always try to control what we do, say and how we do it.

The leader as a communicator must follow certain rules to achieve a positive impact and influence.

1. Be honest: keep in mind that people forgive a lot when there is sincerity and truth, but they will rarely forgive you when they don't feel it. In this day and age, it is harder than ever to lie, it is not worth it. Honesty, transparency and truth are the starting point for effective communication.

2. Be more personal and closer: stop publishing corporate communications and start having corporate conversations, think of it as a dialogue, not a monologue. Don't try to copy other people's communication patterns, keep your own style; your gestures, your accent, your intonation, the way you express yourself etc. and constantly seek dialogue to avoid monologue.

3. Be concrete: simplicity and conciseness are always preferable to complexity, length and confusion. Time has never been a more precious commodity than it is today.

4. Show some vulnerability: historically, leaders seemed indestructible. Today, we know from science and experience that leaders need to express their emotions in order to create a stronger bond with those around them, especially with those they influence. We have become accustomed, for example, to seeing leaders laugh, get angry, or even cry, and this makes them more human. Humanize yourself by connecting with your followers through the "real" feelings you have. Share your emotions to connect with people, but do so with balance and caution.

5. Be open-minded: remember that it is not the opinion that counts, but the willingness to discuss it with an open mind and to learn. Be flexible and responsive to the ideas of others.

6. Shut up and listen: great leaders know when to speak and when to listen. Conversation is a two-way street: listening and

speaking. The ideal communication is a conversation. Great leaders have been great "listeners" and they understood that starting with listening can be extremely beneficial; listening to people's needs, fears, dreams, ambitions etc. can be the starting point to understand them and be able to influence them.

7. Replace ego with empathy: empathetic communicators demonstrate a level of authenticity and transparency that is not present in those who choose to communicate solely with themselves in mind. If you want to connect with people don't talk about yourself, talk about them. It is very difficult to influence people through your ideas but very powerful if you touch what is important to them.

8. Read between the lines: being a leader should not be seen as a license to turn up the volume on rhetoric. Rather, wise leaders know that much more is gained by reading and listening to what is not written or said. Being able to listen to "what is not said" is part of the leader's job. Understand others by reading between the lines. Observe and listen to what is not said.

9. When you speak, make sure you know what you are talking about: develop a technical mastery of your topic. Be prepared, read, research information to speak on a topic. We know that the best way to influence people is to have a technical understanding of what we're talking about, so if necessary, don't be afraid to give definitions, numbers and references etc. Be an expert!

10. Speaking to groups as if they were individuals: even when we are speaking to a group of people (three or a hundred), let's try to speak to the audience as if they were (because they really are!) individuals by looking people in the eye, creating complicity, addressing them by name when we know it, etc.

11. Last point: be prepared to change the message if necessary. Always have a PLAN B. Always. Communication is adapted to reality, not the other way around. The world moves so fast that after preparing a speech or a presentation, five minutes before you start speaking something happens that changes the context: adapt quickly! Keep an eye on the news at all times!

Verbal communication is important, but we know from Albert Mehrabian's famous work in 1971 that the impact of non-verbal communication is the key. Professor Mehrabian mentions the figure of 55% for the part of the impact of our message related to non-verbal language.

These tips can be used for different purposes and in different situations, as we will see below:

- To build trust, pay attention to the following: when you join a conversation between people and greet them for the first time, lean in slightly and shake hands firmly (if sanitary conditions permit!), make good eye contact, with a broad smile, then step back, if they take a step forward towards you, it means they are supportive, if they take a step back or move away a little, they probably want to be somewhere else.

- To influence your peers' behaviors, the most effective way is to first identify your behavioral base by spending some time observing theirs (their arms, torso, hands), then match that behavior to your peers in terms of their hand positions, arm positions, body angles and then slowly introduce your own body language for them to respond to you. Mimicry is fundamental to nonverbal communication.

- To improve communication during a meeting, follow a similar process to the one described above, but briefly stop reflecting the body angle; simply match what you are doing with your hands, head and gestures. This will create a sense of confidence because you will be perceived as "one of them."

- To improve negotiations, you can use body language to capture the underlying power structure in the other team. Identify the leader by observing that when the leader changes position, followers naturally join in and do the same after a short period of time. Identify the "different" person who does not react in the same way or at the same pace. This person will not change their behaviour when the leader does. It can be helpful to know this, just as it can be helpful to work with this person in a different way.

- Create a sense of comfort and ease with your feet, voice and open posture. Then recalibrate once you have observed the reactions of others.

Reflecting on your own body language and learning to control it or project what you want are often untapped techniques for influencing people that any leader might consider developing in order to be influential without others noticing. In short, good nonverbal language would follow these guidelines:

1. Head straight and body open (avoid closed arms and body leaning to the side)

2. Large smile, we know that people who smile inspire more confidence and optimism!

3. Eye contact (maximum 3 seconds) Too much eye contact can be uncomfortable, especially in some cultures.

4. Use your hands to accompany your speech, without using the accusing finger. Hands can be very powerful to accompany our message.

5. Avoid excessive or repetitive movements (such as playing with a pen, moving your leg or drawing on paper) as they can convey boredom and lack of interest).

6. Using the steepling position consists in joining hands (on a table or standing). This position is well known and used by politicians and journalists, and it is a position of control and security. Create a pyramid with your hands.

7. Move around the room to show dynamism: moving around the room during a presentation conveys security and energy. If we can, ideally, we will move from right to left to show our control of the space and not from front to back as this can be perceived as aggressive.

8. Use the power of silence. Make the pause create intrigue, intensity and emotion. Silence can be very powerful in intensifying our message.

## 5. Cooperation / leadership teams

- What is a team: difference between group and team?
- Motivate and correct.
- Create and develop other leaders.

> *"To command is to serve. Neither more nor less."*
> André Malraux

In this chapter, we will address a fundamental issue for the leader: the difference between a group and a team. We will learn what leaders need to do to motivate or correct and how leaders need to be able to identify other leaders and help them develop as leaders.

To understand and know how to work with several people at the same time, we need to differentiate the most commonly used terms:

- A group is a collection of several people who are united to achieve a specific goal, without having a common vision.
- A team is a group of people who contribute their knowledge to achieve the same goal, based on equal support from those who compose it.

Both definitions refer to a social entity formed by a number of people who are part of a company or any other organization in a professional or non-professional environment, and who are differentiated because they have different objectives.

## Leadership: the positive influence

In a group, the people who "create" it do not have a common vision, but each of them, independently, fulfills a specific function. Therefore, the way of working is individual and it is not necessary to have the information of the other members of the group to be able to realize each part.

To understand a working group, you need to see a number of people who meet regularly. Below we list some characteristics of the group:

1. Disjointed.
2. One-dimensional communication.
3. It does not seek consensus.
4. Various affiliations.
5. The leader decides, discusses and delegates.
6. The purpose of the group is the same as the mission of the organization.
7. Individual responsibility.
8. The product of the work is individual.

Based on the following definition of a team: "A team is a small number of people with complementary skills who are committed to a common goal, performance objectives and an approach in which they assume joint responsibility", we will also list some of its most important characteristics:

1. Articulated.
2. Two-dimensional communication.
3. Seek consensus.

4. Strong affiliation.
5. The team decides, discusses and really works together.
6. Shared individual and collective responsibility.
7. The product of this work is a group.
8. The team holds meetings to resolve problems.

> "A team is not a group of people who work together, but a group of people who trust each other."
> Simon Sinek

In a company where employees are teams and not groups, they must meet a number of requirements such as:

- Know the mission: all members must be clear about what they want to achieve and how to get there.
- Sharing of achievements: the people working in the team share information on an ongoing basis. Everyone's contributions add up so that the work created is not the work of one but of all. The achievements are the responsibility of each person in the team.
- Respect: within the team, we must consider others as equals, no one is superior to anyone else, the contributions and ideas of others are equally valid.
- Commitment: if we work as a team, we must keep in mind that our role is important and that we cannot let others down. We must respect our commitments and work in a serious and regulated way.

- Sacrifice: we must keep in mind that we work cooperatively and that what we want will not always be the best or what will be chosen. Sometimes we have to sacrifice our ideas and thoughts to get a greater benefit.
- "I make the difference": in a team, we are all indispensable, we do our part and it is different from the rest. We created this team because we are different and have different skills that together create the magic, we need to make this company successful.

That's why it's essential that if a company is to succeed, the group of people who make up the company work hard to become a team.

The leader must motivate and correct the team, but to do this he must first create the team.

We often find that we do not choose our team and that we have to get to know it in order to get the best out of it. This is the case, for example, of someone who is appointed Minister of Justice of a country and who has not chosen the judges, civil servants, etc., who will be part of his team but who will have to work with them. In this case, the leader will have to "own" his team, get to know them, motivate them and make them want to go in the same direction as him so that they can work together effectively.

To create a team, we need to look for people who are motivated, willing to improve and work comfortably, who like what they are going to do, even if it is not enough. To start the team, the elements mentioned above are very good, but if we stay there, what we will have managed to create is a group, not a team. To prevent this from happening, we need to try to improve communication between members and make them all feel important but at the same time equal within the "group". Not all groups are created in the same way or in the same length of time, each one does it at its own pace because the people who integrate it must get to know each other and integrate at their own pace.

For the team to be good, true and sustainable, we need to learn from the beginning to trust each other and listen to different options and ideas in order to open our minds and learn different ways of doing things and enjoy the process.

The good leader does not only influence, does not only have a good vision and does not only make people go towards his vision but the good leader goes even further, because the good leader will be able to create new leaders. These new leaders must emerge from your own team. As a leader, you have the challenge of getting others on your team to become leaders. Whether internally, for example, if you are a sales manager for a company and you plan to take on other roles in the company soon and you want one of your sales people to be the new sales manager, you will be able to help someone who has the desire and ability to lead.

In contrast to this example, we find another that frequently occurs in politics, where a great leader appears in a political party and the search and preparation of other possible leaders is not cultivated. When this great leader disappears for some reason, the political party is almost extinguished because no one is ready to replace him in his functions. Or in family businesses where the founder is a very charismatic and powerful person who is a very good leader and leaves no room for other leaders. When that person gets older and leaves the position, the company disappears because there is no one ready to take over the leadership role.

A team is composed of a group of people who are part of a common project with a specific objective. In this case, the leader will serve as

*Leadership: the positive influence*

a motivator, guide and reference for the team members. Every team needs a leader to encourage and support it. This leader must be able to confidently guide and reinforce positive thinking at all times to achieve the best possible results. The work developed is created in a cooperative manner where everyone works together and helps each other.

How do you create a team? Here are some guidelines you can follow:
- accept that differences of opinion are part of the process,
- focus on action to achieve common goals,
- actively listen to the form and content of your interviewer,
- give space to other members to show their contributions,
- encourage open discussion and negotiation (the goal is to solve problems collectively).
- It is discussed, decided and worked on together.

*"If a leader doesn't convey passion and intensity, then there won't be any in the organization and people will start to fall off and get depressed."*
Colin Powell

# CHAPTER IV

# THE LEADER AND THE COMPANY

# THE LEADER AND THE COMPANY

## 1. Vision, Strategy and Tactics

- Finding the vision: the long term
- Definition of the strategy: the medium term
- Definition of tactics: the short term

> *"However beautiful the strategy, you should occasionally look at the results."*
> Winston Churchill

In this chapter, we will address another of the fundamental issues of leadership: the leader's vision. We have already emphasized throughout this book that one of the key issues for every leader is his or her vision, the goal he or she has set, the direction he or she wants to take. Without vision, there is no leader. Why would they follow me if I don't know where I'm going?

Let's remember that the leader's starting point and the polar star of the leader is his mission; what is he trying to achieve? This mission cannot be successfully accomplished if we do not have the ability to give content to this mission with the vision.

### Finding the vision: the long term

The leader's vision is a certain anticipation of a better future.

> *"The best way to predict the future is to create it."*
> Peter Drucker

Each leader's vision will tell you what goal he or she wants to achieve and what he or she decides to work tirelessly to achieve. The leader's vision will make him question his reality and launch him into action, into the search for change; the vision is born out of a state of discontent and is not something that can be taught, it is something that must be found. This nonconformity is the beginning of a state of seeking. As long as it is practiced and the search for improvement continues, there will be growth, otherwise it will decline.

The vision will represent a future state to be reached, it is the place where we want to arrive; the attitude of the leader must start from the confidence to believe that it is possible in spite of the obstacles and the adversities and to go forward.

Having a vision is necessary:

Non-conformity + Optimism + Decision = Action

Today, more than ever, leaders and their people are looking for meaning in their work. So, leaders who want to achieve the influence and appeal of their dreams must take this as their starting point:

- Non-compliance - Identify opportunities for improvement in the face of current deficiencies and areas in which to apply those improvements, although not necessarily as a result of errors and expectations of the new competition.
- Optimism - Working to build an environment of trust through the leader's consistency, taking into account that the leader's proposals are examples that he himself practices. This manifests itself in actions that are commensurate with the personal sacrifice that must be made to achieve the desired goal.
- Decision: initiate action by taking tangible steps to make the proposal a reality, using all available means and producing the necessary options to achieve it, even when circumstances are contrary. The leader's optimism in the face of adversity generates confidence and motivation.

This vision is attractive when it is reflected in its social and human impacts, not simply as a bottom-line success, but as something that contributes to humanity, making all people feel like collaborators in a new social order. In addition, the leader presents his or her vision with such humility that it will reinforce his or her vision, his or her credibility, and the solutions to the problems that arise will be seen as challenges and not as problems.

It is important to emphasize that the leader must work to achieve his or her own vision. Vision is not innate and it is not found by chance. Vision is the result of a deep knowledge of reality and a strong capacity and will to change the status quo with an anticipation of the ideal future.

One example: perhaps one of the most famous and inspiring speeches of the 20th century is Martin Luther King's famous "I have a dream" speech delivered in Washington DC on August 28, 1963.

*"I have a dream today! I have a dream that one day, deep in Alabama, with its hate-filled racists - with its governor from whose lips the words of interposition and nullification drip - one day, even there, in Alabama, little black boys and little black girls will be able to go hand in hand with little white boys and little white girls, as brothers and sisters.*

*I have a dream today! I have a dream that one day every valley will be raised and every hill and mountain will be leveled, the rough spots will be leveled and the crooked places will be made straight, and "the Glory of God will be revealed and all that is flesh will see it together".*

The most motivating part of this speech is the fact that it anticipates a better future than the present.

The leader shows his vision as the reason for all the efforts he makes to reach a goal, which is also a reason for working as a team and requires the cooperation and coordination of all its members. The more stimulating the vision is for the present, the stronger it is for his collaborators and the deeper it is, the more transcendent it is.

When we find an opportunity in the market or in a social moment, the charismatic leader will seek to make the most of it. It is a mistake to think that the leader's vision comes to him or her by magic and chance; the process is gradual and is the result of an intense search. The vision that no one can provide, must be found.

How do you find your vision? The leader must build his vision. And building a vision is not something spontaneous and natural. Building a vision is the result of a lot of work and effort. To have a vision, you need to know your country, its economy, its demographics and its history in the case of a public leader; a private sector leader needs to know his industry, his customers, his product, his competitors, the market trends etc. Without these elements, it is impossible to have a vision.

Thus, to ensure the success of the leader's vision, it must be based on his or her thorough knowledge of the realities and limitations of the environment, as well as the opportunities, and empathy with the needs of his or her followers. If the leader is far from reality or does not empathize with his or her people, his or her own vision may become utopian. Quick successes can lead to a distortion of the leader's vision, or to the belief that he or she is infallible and refuses to understand the realities of other points of view. The leader must always be prepared to reorient his or her own vision.

Faced with the phrase "because it's always been done that way" the leader will not accept these obsolete topics; he will ask himself "why not in a different and better way? "This sense of non-conformity is a source of energy for the charismatic leader, who always remains active in looking for opportunities to do more with the same or less. He or she is also impatient, seems to be in a great hurry for things to change in the here and now, always identifying major challenges, although this quickness can become a weakness if it is not consolidated and appropriately posed with each change.

Positive dissatisfaction is a basic ingredient for the life of the company and is an irreplaceable part of its success. The leader must learn to develop and motivate this feeling of optimistic dissatisfaction in his employees, and in the same way, he must project an image of the future that is far superior and better than the current situation.

If we succeed in awakening this attitude, the true sense of improvement will come from it, and the leader will have to become a conscious and constantly motivated person to question the current situation and launch his team in the search for new solutions. The effectiveness of the leader will also be measured by the extent to which he or she succeeds in doing so.

If the vision responds to the long term, it is no less important to take into consideration how the medium and short term allow us to build the path to reach this vision.

### *Definition of the strategy: the medium term*

If you look up the definition of strategy in a dictionary, you will find two possible meanings:

- the art of planning and directing military operations, especially those of war,
- a series of very thoughtful, goal-oriented actions.


In fact, the definition of this strategy is linked to these two ideas, on the one hand, to obtaining the necessary information to overcome an obstacle (I am in A and I want to go to B) and, on the other hand, to the risk of the lack of complete information on how I can get from A to B.

It is impossible to exercise leadership in a company alone. It requires the implementation of strategies to shape and condition it to the needs of each organization, in addition to having a person with certain characteristics and skills.

Leadership strategies are usually built over years and are based on the experience of the people who implement them. That is why we can say that a leader with ten years of experience in the position is not the same as a leader who has been there only a few months. In addition, it is not the same to lead a multinational company that is consolidated in the market as to lead a company that is just taking its first steps.

There are many leaders, but not all have the same degree of effectiveness and influence. The difference between them lies in the decisions they make in their role and in their relationships with their teams.

### *Six strategies to promote it*

Leadership is a reality that can be improved and promoted within a company. Nothing is ever final; on the contrary, everything can be improved. The evolution towards a more effective, influential and optimal leadership model must be a concrete objective for all those who work in these management spheres.

The multiple needs of companies have led to a diversification of strategies to strengthen and promote leadership. In the list below, we detail six of them:

1. **Emotional balance**

   It is essential to learn to keep a cool head. The figure of the angry, frantic leader is now obsolete. Leadership is not reinforced by inflexible decisions that seek to intimidate or generate fear and insecurity. Instead, it is achieved by balancing the emotions that support decisions.

2. **Motivation**

   In situations of low productivity or internal crisis, teams will need the support and motivation of a good leader more than ever. This is a great opportunity to promote this figure and influence employees to generate change.

3. **Justice and balance**

   The leader who conveys justice and balance is admired by those around him. These two qualities are particularly appreciated by work teams, whose functions are constantly evaluated and analyzed. It is the criterion and not the position that must be privileged when weighing the results.

4. **Reduce hierarchies**

   One strategy that will almost always work is to minimize the number of hierarchical positions or ranks that exist within a corporate structure. This is not to say that this is a call for chaos, not at all. It's just about establishing a more direct relationship with the people who make up the teams. The further away the leader shows up, the less identity he or she will have.

5. **Give the example**

    A leader who does the exact opposite of what he or she tells his or her employees will never be loyal to his or her leadership. You have to lead by example. In other words, let's say he talks about planning and its benefits, he can't afford to be late to meetings. Leadership is a quality that must be demonstrated on a daily basis and in the first person.

6. **Reality and optimism**

    Who is willing to follow a leader who has totally lost his sense of opportunity and direction? Leadership will only be strengthened if the decisions to be made are strongly rooted in reality and are achievable.

*Definition of tactics: the short term*

The etymological origin of the word "tactics" comes from the Greek word "taktikos" which derives from the verb "tassain" which means "to order". Tactics is a concept closely related to strategy, which consists of different means (tactics) to achieve an objective. Therefore, we can define tactics as the instruments or tools necessary to execute the plan of action previously conceived in the strategy, ordering the resources available to us and adapting them to the circumstances.

We talk about tactics when we talk about the short term, what needs to be done to make the strategy possible.

Seven examples of tactics that can help us.

1. **Don't be the first to respond**

    Listen before you speak. Express to your team that you expect truths and concrete answers. Don't settle for a yes or no, look for the why in others' answers.

2. **Share all information**

    Share the information with your employees, even if you think they already know about it. The way you present the information can lead to a different approach and therefore a better solution.

3. **Appreciate the positive reaction**

    For example, say to the person you are talking to, "I didn't expect that answer, what did you base it on? "It's best to backtrack a bit.

4. **Change your perception of things**

    A leader once told me that he never held meetings without knowing what the outcome would be. I continued to avoid his meetings, why? Once people around you realize that it doesn't really matter what they say, they will stop telling you what they really think.

5. **Ask concrete and key questions**

   There is nothing more frustrating for a leader than having to listen to things that are not relevant. Exposing your doubts about what you hear is motivating and encourages people to prepare for meetings and discussions.

6. **Act on constructive disagreement with cordiality**

   Sometimes, differences considered constructive will be presented and rejected, in this case, show your disagreement without being unpleasant and be cordial with this person.

7. **Make decisions**

   Discussions that do not result in a decision are demoralizing and lead to frustration. People want to participate and they want leaders to make responsible decisions that define and mark a clear direction for their future.

Thus, to conclude this chapter, we see how a fundamental part of the leader's job is to be able to manage the long, medium and short term. In other words: anticipating the future (having a vision, in the long term), identifying the necessary paths to achieve that vision (the strategy, in the medium term) and finally knowing the next steps to take to make that strategy operational (the tactics, in the short term).

## 2. Customer orientation

- The changing role of the client in recent years
- 10 techniques that will help us make the customer experience the main philosophy
- The diversity of clients

> *"By far the #1 factor that has contributed to our success is this compulsive obsession we have with focusing on the customer, rather than the competition".*
> Jeff Bezos

We will now talk about the changing role of the customer in recent years. A few years ago, there was a revolution in the product concept (product-centric business). Companies built their strategies around the product concept, which not only had to be good, but also the design had to be beautiful. Later, there was a new revolution with the service that was given to customers (company service) and now companies are customer-centric, why? Because today the customer has acquired a fundamental importance, the customer has a power that he never had before, whether in B2B or in B2C the customer now has much more information than before, much more volatility than before, much more ability to choose, much more ability to change, etc.

For example, to travel 30 years ago, you had no choice but to go to a travel agency. In the best case, the person who received you would show you catalogs with pictures of the hotels and services they had and you would decide. Nowadays, when you plan a trip, you can search a lot of information about the place, follow the recommendations of the hotels through social networks, make comments, see hundreds of pictures, etc. this makes the customer much more demanding.

Today, companies that want to be successful must be much more customer oriented and who says companies says leaders. Leaders today have to be 100% customer oriented and we all have customers; every business is someone's supplier and someone else's customer. What is important is that we take into account this definition of the customer, who is our customer? The customer is the one who can decide to buy or not our product or service, the customer is the real boss of the company. And this customer can be internal or external but he has the power to choose us or not. In a way, without customer there is no company, without customer there is no real need of leader.

We would point out that this term is not as new as it sounds, since Lester Wunderman, the creator of modern direct marketing, developed this idea as early as 1967, but it is only relatively recently that companies have put it into practice.

The strategy of "customer orientation" is to put the customer at the center of everything, to be customer-centric and to develop a strategy in which product-company-customer services are united and aligned in order to achieve significant benefits.

The customer must be at the center of our product because it is the consumers who will buy and use it, if they are not taken into consideration, they will think they are not important to us. A customer needs trust and security in the company, they want us to give them the feeling that we care about them, so if we can't give it to them directly, it's through our product that this feeling of care must be reflected. We have to do things for our customers, and it's not up to the customers to adapt to what we do, as has been the case so far.

Below is a list of 10 techniques that will help us make the customer experience the core philosophy of our business and help us create a customer-centric environment throughout your organization.

1. **Set customer-centric values**

    It is essential to establish that, as companies, we must follow customer-centric values. Visualize the goal in your mind. Identify what your customer's experience should be, and then design the path to reach that goal.

    Promote empathy as a value among your employees. Empathy is the ability to understand the customer's needs, to identify their emotions and the reasons for these needs in order to respond effectively to their problems.

2. **Integrate them into your culture**

    Once the basic customer experience philosophy is established, promote the awareness and philosophy of putting the customer first. Conduct training sessions for new employees and refresher sessions for existing employees, disseminate these values through posters and communications to ensure that the customer experience is a priority.

3. **Give priority to customer satisfaction**

   Customers keep your company running and are the key stakeholders in your business. When it comes to dealing with customer issues, your employees must put customer satisfaction above all else. This may mean reworking schedules, occasionally sacrificing profits, or rescheduling meetings to manage and/or respond to customers.

4. **Ownership of shares**

   Everyone is responsible for ensuring a successful customer experience: leaders, executives, technical, marketing and sales teams must all take responsibility for delivering a consistent and enhanced customer experience.

5. **Contract by customer value**

   The employees who carry out your day-to-day operations have a significant impact on how customers perceive your brand. When hiring, candidates should be evaluated on their skills, attitude, customer focus and personality. They should be a good fit for your culture. This is the time to check people's empathy and orientation.

6. **Listen to your customer's voice**

   Listening to the customer facilitates interactions with customers to gather their opinions, criticisms and suggestions for improving services and products. Facilitates interactions between employees and customers to identify their achievements and challenges.

This will allow your team to establish a good rapport with the customer and better understand their requirements.

7. **Train and prepare employees**

   Companies and organizations must empower their employees to go beyond the call of duty to better serve the customer. Employees must be empowered to make on-the-spot decisions that exceed customer expectations and should not be constrained by internal policies. Provide your employees with tools, guidance and space to solve customer problems.

8. **Create a positive experience for your employees**

   Because an empowered employee is a happy employee. When you expect your employees to deliver, it's important to treat them well. In fact, it's very important to equip them with the right tools and technology to make the customer experience more enjoyable.

9. **Measure results with clients**

   You can't do better when you can't measure it.

   As a company, you need to be able to measure the impact of your efforts on the customer experience, and link customer satisfaction to employee incentive and compensation programs. When employees have a vested interest in customer satisfaction, they are better aligned to deliver a better customer experience.

**10. Reward and celebrate success with clients**

When an employee strives to exceed customer expectations, they should be recognized and rewarded. Recognition and reward will serve as motivation for everyone to continue and do better in the future.

If clients find value in your services, celebrate it and share your success to appreciate and inspire your employees.

It is important to focus on product and sales, but customer focus must be a priority for both leaders and employees. It is prudent to make customer centricity and empathy core values. Align with leaders who champion and practice these values in the organization and empower employees to deliver a better customer experience.

In addition to all of the above and to put it in context, we must try to make creating unique and complete things for our customers the primary focus of the company. To do this, we need to consider the diversity of the customers we have. Not all customers are the same. They will not provide the same returns to our company and they will not have the same needs.

It is fundamental to know how to differentiate and classify them according to certain parameters that allow us to observe values such as commitment, quality, need, etc., of the customers; to know for which customers we should make more commercial efforts, which customers we should take care of in more detail, in which customers and with whom we should invest more efforts, but always without leaving aside the rest of the customers, because they are also necessary for the functionality of the company.

It is essential to be able to listen at all times and find new ways to serve the most valuable customers in a meaningful way. If we can do this, it will help us achieve greater profitability for the company or organization.

Given the diversity of customers, the value that will be applied to each of them is different. Therefore, we will try to plan, according to our possibilities, the commercial and marketing efforts we can make, taking into account the people we want to address in order to always face the right customers. In order to do this, we need to create or use a system to obtain information about the needs, feelings and tastes of customers.

It is essential that the customer feels loved and important within the commercial circle. We must establish a favorable direct communication, and if this is not possible, we must try that through our product, this is reflected so that the customer feels well served at all times (special offers, satisfaction surveys or share with him the products that interest him).

That said, any leader who wants to apply this strategy in his or her company must make all employees understand that the company's mission is to satisfy the concrete needs of customers better than other competitors and not to worry about selling what they produce without considering who the buyer will be.

## 3. Risks and decision making

- What risk is and what leaders do with it: anticipation.
- Decision making.
- Accepting mistakes: perseverance.

> *"The biggest risk is not taking risks... In a world that is changing very quickly, the only strategy that is guaranteed to fail is not to take risks."*
> Mark Zuckerberg

In this chapter we will discuss a very important issue when we talk about leadership: risk and decision making, every leader has to make decisions and risks, risk cannot be cancelled and is everywhere but we have to learn to anticipate it, to mitigate it and if possible, to control it.

Bringing up the subject of risk and decision making after the experience we had with the Covid crisis seems more relevant than ever. The leader must master these two concepts: risk and decision making.

We have to keep in mind that the risk is not only negative, for example, imagine that a regular customer buys 1,000 units a month of one of our products and suddenly tells us that he wants 10,000 units next month. What happens? It's great news because he'll buy a very large quantity from us and we'll sell more, but it's also a risk because we may not be ready to produce such a large quantity and it may cause a crisis with the customer.

It is important to know that risk exists and must be assumed, it is endogenous, that is to say that it can come from within the company because we make a mistake or exogenous, because it comes from outside, for example, there is a serious pandemic or an economic crisis that can affect my company.

As Sun Tzu says in the Art of War: *"He who foresees the risk is no longer found"*. Leaders are aware that the risk exists but they take it upon themselves to minimize the consequences of this risk.

Taking risks is part of leadership because leaders often operate in a context of crisis. The world is complex and sometimes dangerous. Risk is part of the life of a company, the life of a leader and the life of a person, but these risks must not be taken just for the sake of it, risks must correspond to a series of criteria for the leader to take meaningful risks:

1. You can take the risks you consider as a leader, but these risks must obviously be for the benefit and in the direction of your company's mission. For example, imagine a regional manager who has a geographical scope established in Italy and who takes risks in France, it would not make sense.

2. You have to accept that when you take a risk, you can win, but sometimes you can lose and pay a price. If you are not willing to pay that price if you lose, you might as well not take the risk.

3. In some cases, it may be better not to take a risk. You will still be a leader for not taking a risk. In fact, one might ask if sometimes the risk is not to take it, and it is perfectly normal

that at some point someone decides not to take that risk and to assume the consequences. Being a leader does not mean taking risks but also deciding not to take them. For example, when Warren Buffet was asked about the secret of his success, he answered that he was able to say no to projects he didn't believe in or didn't want to invest in. So, he didn't take risks all the time and when he decided to take them, it was because he knew it was a good opportunity.

4. Taking a risk has a price and, even if we sometimes get what we want, we will certainly have paid a price for taking that risk.

5. Sometimes the reward takes a long time to come. In some cases, the reward takes so long that we don't even see it. In other words, sometimes as a leader you take a risk and pay the price, but the reward is seen by your successor(s). For example, a lot of the infrastructure and things that we have in our countries today were decided by our parents or grandparents and they didn't see the benefit, we did: building a train line, an aqueduct.

> *"I learned that courage is not the absence of fear, but the ability to overcome it the triumph over it."*
> Nelson Mandela

### Types of risks

Risk can be of several types, the first thing that the leader must do is to anticipate this risk, make an assessment of potential risks and in this sense, we can find different types of risks, very varied depending on the company:

- Time: lack of time, being in a hurry, we could rush without taking the necessary time,
- Communication: lack of good communication can lead to misunderstandings,
- Poorly defined project scope can affect project planning and close-out date,
- Costs, due to poor budgeting or unanticipated expenses,
- Resources needed, poorly planned or anticipated,
- Environment, natural disasters or consequences of climate change.

It is therefore important to take them all into account so that we can prepare ourselves.

### Risk assessment:

What every leader needs to do to prepare for these risks is to assess them, put them on the table and analyze them.

> *"The greatest danger in times of turbulence is not the turbulence, it is to act with yesterday's logic."*
> Peter Drucker

### *Risk analysis matrix:*

Once this risk assessment is done, we need to prepare this risk analysis matrix to calculate the impact and probability. For example: if a risk has a very high impact rate and the probability is very high, it is better not to assume it.

| IMPACT | | LOW | MEDIUM | HIGH |
|---|---|---|---|---|
| SIGNIFICANT | | Considerable management required<br><br>Risk level 7 | Must manage and monitor risks<br><br>Risk level 8 | Extensive management essential<br><br>Risk level 9 |
| MODERATE | | Risk may be worth accepting, with monitoring<br><br>Risk level 4 | Management effort worthwhile<br><br>Risk level 5 | Management effort required<br><br>Risk level 6 |
| MINOR | | Accepts Risks<br><br>Risk level 1 | Accept, but monitor risks<br><br>Risk level 2 | Manage and monitor risks<br><br>Risk level 3 |

**LIKELIHOOD OF ADVERSE EVENT OUTCOME**

In short, we need to do risk identification, risk assessment, risk analysis, and we may need to do a second risk assessment. It's basically a closed circle of:

- potential risks,
- what are the chances of this happening?
- what should I do?

***Decision making***

By definition, the leader must make decisions, but these decisions are not made randomly. A balance must be found between reason and emotion. Most of the decisions we make are not spontaneous, but are studied and premeditated decisions, they are the result of conditions we have around us. We must be aware that making random decisions is not a good way to decide what to do, and even less so if we are dealing with really serious and important issues where the stakes are crucial. The worst enemy in decision making is ourselves, our emotions, our ego and our haste. This is why the leader must not make decisions in a random, improvised or hasty manner. Every leader must be aware of what he or she is facing, look at what is in front of him or her and make an assessment, because decision making is a structured process that requires an analysis of the situation. And that analysis involves constantly asking: what is our vision and where do we want to go?

The leader's duty is to choose what will be the best decision for the company, he is the one who has the vision of the future but must always make the decision from an objective point of view, he takes a responsibility that is for him, for his company and for his supporters. To make this choice, he must evaluate different aspects, there are different decision matrices.

Making decisions in complex situations is never easy, but companies can't afford to make mistakes. Here are 5 points to measure competence when making critical decisions:

1. Identify critical factors that will affect the outcome of a decision. Being a highly skilled decision maker requires excellent interpretive and analytical skills that are used to

identify issues and report on the preparation and implementation phases.

2. Evaluate options accurately and set priorities. Effective leaders can assess the quality of the alternatives and explain the reasons for that assessment.

3. They anticipate outcomes and foresee logical consequences. Expert strategists perform logical analyses in a precise and defined manner in tightly structured contexts. This allows you to see the applications and implications of all the factors that shape and constrain your decision making. Government regulations, policies, fundamentals and protocols must be considered.

4. It measures risk and uncertainty. The most expert managers judge the most uncertain contexts to be anticipatory.

5. She reasons well in contexts that require quantitative analysis. Leaders must be able to analyze, interpret and evaluate key aspects by presenting information in graphs, charts, diagrams, etc. Leaders must understand the meaning of numbers and the impact they will have on their decisions.

Example: if I have a flight from Los Angeles to Paris, I will probably get to the airport early so I don't miss my flight. I'll try to get to the airport early enough to get there safely and I'll take a mode of transportation that I know is safe to arrive on time. Because I know that the risk of missing the plane is serious, because there may be only one flight a day, because I will have a significant financial penalty if I miss it, or because in Paris I am expected to do something specific at a certain time and if I miss that flight I will not arrive on time. On the other hand, another example, if I have a dinner date with friends, I decide that I will take the metro and if I miss it, nothing will happen because the next metro will pass in a few minutes and the only thing that will happen is that I will be a little late for dinner, the risk is not serious.

It is important to assess the risk of the decisions I am about to make.

> *"No leader deserves to be called that if he is not prepared to assume responsibility on the most decisive occasions."*
> Henry Kissinger

### Perseverance: the most powerful leadership trait.

If the leader does not achieve his or her goal at first, he or she must be persistent and keep trying. Leaders do not always succeed on the first try and must work and insist on achieving their goals.

More than effort, perseverance is an instinct that generates the determination to never give up. The persevering leader has a mindset that refuses to accept failure. A persistent leader is one who is willing to endure success over the long term.

Below I share 7 characteristics of persistent leaders:

1. **Definition of purpose**

   Have you ever wondered why you do a certain thing? We only persevere when the answer to that why is strong enough. Nietzsche said, looking at the Nazi concentration camps, that he who has a reason to live can endure almost anything. Your "why" serves as a constant motivation to persevere.

2. **I hope so**

   You have to really want something. Sometimes you don't want something bad enough to make it work. For example, I want to help fight climate change and I'm doing my part by trying to take my car as little as possible to pollute less, but if my desire isn't strong enough, I'll probably continue to use my car to run meaningless errands.

3. **Self-confidence**

   You must truly believe that you have the skills and abilities to achieve the outcome you set out to achieve. For example, if you have to give an important speech and you constantly have doubts about the content you are going to say or your ability to do it well, this lack of confidence will probably cause you to do it badly.

4. **Define your plan**

   If you don't know where you are going, how can you get there? You need to have a structured plan that is as detailed as possible so that you can persevere and stick to it.

5. **Clarification**

   Your persistence must be based on knowledge. It is important to have expert advice and support to ensure that we have all the information we need and that our persistence is focused.

6. **Power**

   Lack of willpower is the main obstacle to the persistence of the disease.

   This will can be defined as follows:
   - the ability to delay getting the award, resisting in the short term to achieve better long-term goals.
   - the ability to override an unwanted thought and turn it around.

   In one rather illuminating example, a group of children were given a lot of candy and it was explained to them that if they didn't eat the candy, they would get more as a reward, but if they ate it right away, they wouldn't get more. Those who showed the greatest willingness to not eat the candy got the highest scores.

## 7. Routine

Perseverance is a direct result of routine. Our mind reflects what it absorbs daily with our routines. If we repeat acts of courage, we will overcome our fears more quickly.

We have several examples to illustrate the perseverance of the leader. For example, the presidents of the French Republic, François Mitterrand and Jacques Chirac, or also the American President Joe Biden ran twice each and lost the presidential elections before being elected on the third attempt, or also the singer Bruce Springsteen, who had to release several albums before becoming a successful author. His first two albums were commercial failures, the third earned him excellent reviews, but it wasn't until the fifth that he got the international recognition he deserved and with the seventh that he became a universal star. If he had thrown in the towel with the second album, he would not have become the star he is today.

## 4. Value creation, problem solving and innovation

- The leader solves problems, divergent or convergent
- The leader creates value
- The leader innovates

> *"Innovation is what distinguishes a leader from a follower."*
> Steve Jobs

In this chapter, we will discuss the idea that the leader, as such, aims primarily at achieving his vision, his objective, his challenge. However, on the road he must travel to reach his goal, he will find a series of obstacles that will prevent him from executing. Faced with these obstacles or barriers, it is essential that the leader has the tools to create value, solve problems and have enough creativity to develop his strategy and reach a positive conclusion. In the end, the leader is nothing more than a problem solver. All problems have solutions, or they really aren't problems.

Imagine that you are coordinating a project and that everything is ready and in place:

- You have a contract, a program, a budget, an agenda, etc., everything is very complete.
- You have defined the objectives with the leaders and the rest of the team members.

- You feel like you are ready and have everything under control.

Halfway through the project, a team member comes to you and suggests a change because they think they have found a better way to manage a part of the process.

You don't like the idea! You are the director not the coordinator! And then someone comes along and advises you to change the direction of the flawless plan you've spent hours and hours preparing. You think this change will only bring you trouble.

This is a common thing for project managers. When you feel solely responsible and have worked hard to get this project off the ground, it's only natural that you feel confident in the process you've put in place and want to maintain it.

But think about it for a moment: perhaps with your negative attitude towards change, you are limiting the flexibility of the rest of the team members who need to move the project forward to another level. By planning every inch of flexibility with extreme precision, you make it difficult to adapt to new information and possible changes that may occur.

So, what can you do? As a leader, the time has come for you to not only think of yourself as a project manager, but to try to get the best out of your teams as well. To do this, leaders must encourage and embrace two concepts of the creative problem-solving process: convergent and divergent thinking.

But what is the difference between convergent and divergent thinking?

Divergent thinking is the process of perceiving and taking on new ideas and possibilities without objection, analysis or discussion. It is this type of thinking that will allow you to freely associate, develop and debate new possible ways to solve complex challenges that have no single answer.

For example, you can think of organizing a brainstorming session, in which you meet to discuss the problem that the company must then address. The participants make all sorts of proposals and suggestions, some of which are even known in advance to be unworkable. This is divergent thinking. You throw out ideas without control or restriction, whether they are useful or not.

Once you have a long list of new goals, what happens? In an ideal world, convergent thinking occurs.

### *And what is convergent thinking?*

Convergent thinking is that which seems to be associated with analysis, reason, wisdom and decision making. This type of thinking involves taking many ideas and ranking them, evaluating them, analyzing the pros and cons, and making decisions based on this organization.

Some of these ideas will be removed from the list because it will quickly become apparent that they are not feasible, either because they are too costly, too slow, require too many resources, or simply because they are too far from reality. We can therefore summarize convergent thinking as the process of sifting through ideas to find the solution.

If we contrast convergent thinking with divergent thinking: is one better than the other?

Everyone has the ability to adopt both convergent and divergent thinking, depending on the situation. However, it is common to lean more towards one or the other when dealing with different problems or projects as they arise.

People who are naturally inclined to think outside the box are those in the organization who like to come up with new ideas. They are the most effective at solving large and complicated problems because they are the most likely to develop new and useful ideas.

The problem is relying too much on one of the two methods of thinking. Too much divergent thinking can lead to endless ideas and no solutions, and too much convergent thinking can lead to no new ideas and stagnation in the analysis process.

### *How to encourage more divergent thinking*

While leaders must encourage teams to think differently, setting deadlines is still essential to being more effective. How do you find the balance?

How can we incorporate divergent thinking into project planning processes and be creative without creating chaos?

We'll discuss a series of tips that will give you the skills to adapt quickly to changes and new demands without anything going wrong.

1. **You must allow sufficient time for both types of reflection**

   Both convergent and divergent thinking are important for creative problem solving and project planning, which means setting aside enough time for each and not rushing.

   Trying to think divergently and convergently at the same time is counterproductive, mixing the two thoughts at the same time is like putting on the gas and the brake at the same time. It will get us nowhere.

   While both types of thinking are necessary for success, it is smartest and most effective to separate them. Start by educating project team members about both types of thinking.

   When you start a brain storming session, insist that this time the session is for divergent thoughts only. No idea is too big or absurd; everything will be valued. Remind the other contributors that this is not the time to oppose each other's proposals.

   This will ensure that you give people enough space to think outside the box, before moving directly to planning. 38% of employees admit that leaders rejecting ideas without first analyzing them is a reason why they often don't dare to take the initiative; therefore, divergent thinking will not only improve project results, but also build self-esteem.

2. **Propose and implement a collaborative work management system.**

   A collaborative project management platform (such as Teams, for example) is a great way to provide constant and immediate visibility into project planning and progress. This type of work system also provides the flexibility to encourage differences of opinion.

Real-time mentions and comments promote collaboration around big ideas without having to schedule meetings or link information across multiple email threads. Flexible folder structures and custom fields allow project managers to quickly implement new project templates and process workflows.

In short, a good collaborative work management platform makes it easy to replicate what works well, but also gives you the flexibility to think differently and adapt to changing goals and demands.

3. **Forget about the small details.**

No one has time to think creatively when it comes to constant updates, assignments and project development. Project managers often save time by moving directly to convergent thinking.

Fortunately, we now have technology tools that can free up project managers and help teams get rid of the most annoying administrative tasks. For example, simply removing the need to manually assign task owners, create project templates, or send status update notifications will already be a release.

By minimizing the heaviest repetitive work, teams will have more time to move on to divergent thinking that might otherwise have taken a back seat. Offload the entire planning and process part to technology and focus only on what technology can't do for you.

Can you plan and be creative? The answer is yes. Planning and creativity seem to be mutually exclusive, but when you learn the secrets of divergent and convergent thinking, you will realize that both can achieve something great.

There is room and time for both, and the most effective leaders know when and how to use them effectively.

If you follow the tips, we've discussed here, you'll be able to keep projects under control and, in addition to being flexible and agile, you'll be open to change and appreciate new ideas.

Leadership, without a doubt, is a creative way of thinking and relating to people and situations, while serving as a guide and example for others.

To stay creative and open to new ideas as a leader, it is interesting and helpful to learn more about divergent thinking, as leaders who embrace divergent thinking offer great advantages.

Thus, at this point, we think the difference between the two types of thinking is clear, obviously one diverges and the other converges. One is open and unbiased; the other is critical and chooses to limit the process to one selection option. But this does not mean that these seemingly opposite ways of thinking cannot work together.

It is helpful to have an open mind at the beginning, and then focus during the decision-making process. Some leaders can move seamlessly from one way of thinking to another, but more often than not, leaders are more inclined to one of two mindsets or thoughts. It is important to understand that divergent and convergent thinking can coexist, cooperate and thrive.

It's clear that companies that don't take risks won't move forward. That's just the way it is. We live in a time of constant and very rapid change. There are technological disruptions, interconnectivity, etc. But all of this requires a new way of looking at things, assimilating them and looking for solutions and methods to move forward. This is where divergent thinking stands out the most: it is creative, inherent and often innovative.

Here are some formulas for triggering divergent thinking to work toward better leadership:

- Think it through: take time to think, observe and consider something. Seek out information and gather the data you need to understand the context of the problem, but then take as much time as you need to see what comes out. Don't be afraid to share ideas with the team. Remember that no idea is wrong, even if it seems contradictory at first.

- Run first, then improve: divergent thinking does not mean being indecisive. Moreover, as far as experimentation is concerned, you will see what happens, instead of being sure that the right path is the one that comes from traditional means and the one we used. It's about doing it carefully, but not conservatively, and being attentive to what comes up.

- Comments: don't work alone. Divergent thinking is a group activity. But this concept goes beyond brain storming. To use divergent thinking collaborate with your team to facilitate an environment where new ideas can emerge without fear. Embrace a new culture of innovation, don't be afraid of change.

- Invest in yourself as well: it is not only the team that needs nourishment, but also the leader. Divergent thinkers are not complacent, but curious, and are constantly seeking improvement. They seek to grow and continue to learn by attending frequent training and coaching sessions. Take online courses, read self-help books, etc.

- Involve your team: as a leader, you need to maintain frequent communication with your team, both formal and informal. Having a group of divergent thinkers and a leader who uses divergent thinking will develop creativity and ideas exponentially. This can be facilitated by online collaboration tools.

Now let's comment on some examples of divergent thinking to get a better idea of what a divergent thinker is, let's use an example by asking two questions. An easy way to understand the difference between divergent and convergent thinking is to consider the differences between answering an essay question and a multiple-choice question.

The convergent thinker uses a more structured way of thinking, such as a multiple-choice question, where there are incorrect answers that can be discarded to leave the single answer, which is correct.

A divergent thinker, on the other hand, would not phrase the question in this way. The divergent thinker will answer the question more openly. Rather, it is an essay where there is no right answer, and whatever the answer is, it will not be right. The answer lies in taking the time to think before you act. It is a more creative approach to finding a solution.

Another example is that when something is not working, the convergent thinker is more likely to decide that it is time to replace it. It may be the right choice, but it is decided without evaluating other possibilities. The divergent thinker will want to know if there is something that has been done wrong that can be corrected and will "gamble" to do so.

Leadership is no different. If divergent thinking is not a leader's preferred option, it is certainly a very powerful tool that can help someone look beyond what they think they know. It can help them move beyond their comfort zone to appreciate other innovative solutions when necessary.

Divergent thinking leaders are curious, observant and open to new ways of doing things and with this thinking, they will constantly look for new tools to help them work more creatively.

### *Problem solving.*

> *"The way we see the problem is the problem."*
> Stephen R. Covey

The leader must be a professional problem solver, otherwise he or she will not be able to achieve the vision.

The Covid crisis and previous financial, health or security crises have shown how complicated the road can be.

Here are some of the key skills that can help you solve problems effectively:

- **Professionalism at all times**

    The best leaders never lose their cool, even when it seems like all the possible factors for losing their cool and panicking are present. This is especially important when you start building a team. If you stay calm, you will keep the rest of the team calm. By remaining a true professional no matter what, you will earn the respect of everyone from your clients to the team members.

- **Think big**

    A successful entrepreneur always keeps an eye on the big picture, analyzing how it will help them achieve their mission. It can be too easy to get caught up in the little things that come up every day, without thinking beyond the current crisis. It's important for entrepreneurs to tackle the issues and move forward, rather than obsessing over the little things and getting stuck.

    If you focus on the problem of the day, think about how it will affect your business in the long run. You may decide to adapt your approach to problems to ensure the future success of your business, rather than just putting out fires and thinking short-term.

- **Avoid pointing fingers**

    When a problem first appears, it's easy to get caught up in the blame game. You could spend hours trying to identify the team member who made a mistake that led you to the current problem. However, your time will be much more productive if you work with your team to find a solution. Instead of berating your staff and affecting team morale, going into problem-solving mode can make your colleagues feel like they are helping to repair the damage, which will increase their commitment.

- **Collect data**

    Technology has given companies the power to generate volumes of data in almost every aspect of their organization. This information is particularly valuable and helps us identify customer behaviour. Leaders who simply make guesses and assumptions will not outperform their competitors, as other organizations will use data-driven problem-solving methods.

- **Be positive**

    Living in the negative will only affect morale. Instead, be the kind of leader who sees problems as "opportunities" and focus on the positive aspects of solving the problem. If you have a staff meeting, convene groups of people for a brainstorming session. An effective leader does not just work with problems. If you are able to see them as an opportunity to open the lines of communication and involve your team in the solution, you will likely find that your entire company benefits.

- **Follow-up of the results**

    The best way to become a leader is to pay close attention to the outcome of any decision you make. This will help you move forward, providing you with the information you need to run your business in the future. When you know the cause of the problem and how it was resolved, you can also find ways to prevent it from happening in the future.

Leading means handling the day-to-day operations of a business, as well as working to grow and add new revenue. When you are able to properly manage the challenges you face along the way, you are more likely to improve your team's morale, which usually translates into happier customers and more revenue.

Problem solving is the greatest facilitator of growth and opportunity. That's why they say failure is the best lesson in business and in life. Be the leader who demonstrates maturity, acts with courage and takes responsibility. Applying each of these lessons can help you become an example of problem solving. Every experience teaches us new things.

"Impossible *only means that you haven't found the solution yet.*"
Anonymous

# CONCLUSION

# CONCLUSION

The 20 characteristics of a leader:

1. **Trust**

   A leader gains followers and inspires trust by having a clear vision, showing empathy, and being a good professional by the example of their actions. The leader must sometimes demonstrate an assertive attitude without losing the generosity and kindness necessary to earn respect.

2. **Transparency**

   As a leader, the only way to earn your team's trust is to be 100% authentic, open, sometimes flawed but always passionate about your work. You need to be present and real so that your team knows what to expect from you.

3. **Vision**

   To be a great leader, you can't focus on the little things and you can't be distracted from what you're about. To deal with critical situations, you must be able to develop an ability to ignore the unimportant and focus on the big picture and the long term. Otherwise, the trivial will suffocate you.

## 4. Passion

Whatever you do, do it with passion. A leader must know his or her passions well in order to build a speech based on truth. This will lead his followers to the easiest way to achieve their goals. Without passion, the leader becomes an abstract being, without illusion and without direction.

## 5. Inspiration

Leaders do not make themselves; they are always motivated by someone or something, it can come from other leaders, a book, any other reason. Great leaders also have models to follow, referents, but be careful to choose the best ones so as not to follow a wrong inspiration.

## 6. Patience

Patience is really the courage that comes from testing your commitment to your cause. Sometimes the path to great things is difficult, but the best leaders know when to give up on a cause and when to keep rowing. If your vision is bold enough, there will be hundreds of reasons why you won't be able to achieve your goal and you will face many skeptics.

## 7. Stoicism

It is inevitable that we will be faced with very difficult situations, whether due to costly mistakes, unforeseen events or unscrupulous enemies. Stoicism is originally about accepting and anticipating so that we don't scare ourselves, react emotionally badly, or make the situation even worse.

Training our mind, imagining worst-case scenarios and controlling our unnecessary reactions is the way to prevent these complicated situations from becoming fatal.

8. **Analysis**

   Understanding our company's figures and reality is the best information we can get for our business. Having applications that provide us with all types of data in the form of balance sheets, graphs, statistics and knowing how to interpret them, will be very valuable information for any manager.

9. **Authenticity**

   It is true that imitation is one of the greatest forms of flattery, but not when it comes to leadership, because any great leader must be authentic. There is value in learning from others, learning from the biographies of other leaders, and gaining skills along the way, but never losing your voice, opinion, or essence

10. **An open mind**

    One of the great myths is that good business leaders are visionaries who have a strong determination to follow their goals no matter what. This is not the case. The truth is that leaders need to keep an open mind and be flexible to adjust their strategy as needed. When you are in the start-up phase, planning takes a back seat and your goals are not concrete, your goal should be to develop good relationships.

## 11. Ability to delegate

The most effective teams are not always the most talented, but they do have the right mix of skills and the ability to rely on their teammates. Building a successful team requires delegating responsibility and authority, which is not always easy. This is the only way to discover the true capabilities of your people and get the most out of them.

## 12. Generosity

We all grow as a team, as a collective when we help others to grow as individuals. The leader's victory is collective and no leader reaches the top alone.

## 13. Persistence

All things take time and you have to persist, always. That's what makes you a good leader, the willingness to go beyond what might stop others.

## 14. Communication

If people don't know your expectations and don't meet them, you are actually to blame for not communicating well. It is essential to establish good communication with the people you work with; communication is a balancing act. You may have a very specific need, but you need to view the work as a collaborative effort.

## 15. Responsibility

It is much easier to blame someone than to accept some responsibility when things have not gone well. Accepting blame, owning up to the mistake and doing something about the impact is a responsibility.

## 16. Restlessness

It takes real leadership to find the strengths of each team member and then look outside to fill in the gaps. You have to believe that your team doesn't have all the answers on its own, because if you think they do, you're not asking the right questions.

## 17. Positive Attitude

To achieve greatness, you must create a culture of optimism. There will be many ups and downs, but if positivity prevails, it will help your business move forward. Remember, though, that this takes courage. You have to truly believe that your team can do the impossible.

## 18. Authenticity

We all notice when someone is not authentic. The more you focus on building authentic connections with your people, the more likable you will be in the eyes of others. You don't have to be a great leader, but you do have to be more respected, which can be a huge positive for your business or project.

## 19. Decision-making capacity

Often you have to make decisions quickly and without the ability to react. Sometimes a bad decision can give you better results in the long run and build a stronger team than a correct decision made in haste.

## 20. Integrity

Our people are a direct reflection of the values we hold dear as leaders. If we always want to be right, we limit our team's potential to the maximum and lose talent. If we emphasize integrity in all of our interactions, it will permeate the culture of our company.

# BIBLIOGRAPHY

# BIBLIOGRAPHY

- Aurelius, Marcus, "Meditations", Independently Published 2021
  Aristotle, "The Art of Rhetoric", Oxford University Press, 2018
- Anderson and Adams, "Mastering Leadership," Wiley, 2015
- Anderson and Adams, "Scaling Leadership," Wiley, 2019
- Blanchard & Johnson, "The New One Minute Manager "Simon & Schuster 2001
- Bossidy and Charan, "Execution: The Discipline of Getting Things Done," Crown -Business, 2002
- Bregman, "Leading with Emotional Courage," Wiley, 2018
- Bennis, "On Becoming a Leader", Basic Books, 2009
- Brown, Brené, "Braving the Wilderness," Random House, 2017
- Brown, Brené, "Dare to Lead," Random House, 2018
- Carnegie, Dale, "How to Win friends and influence people", Simon & Schuster, Ed. 2009
- Cialdini, Robert, "Influence The Psychology of Persuasion", Harper Business, Expanded Edition 2021
- Christensen, "How Will You Measure Your Life?" HarperCollins, 2012
- Christensen, "Competing Against Luck," HarperBusiness, 2016

- Chomsky, Noham, "The Essential Chomsky", The New Press, 2008
- Collins and Porras, "Built to Last," HarperBusiness, 1994
- Collins, "Good to Great," HarperBusiness, 2001
- Collins, "How the Mighty Fall," HarperCollins, 2009
- Collins and Hansen, "Great by Choice," HarperCollins, 2011
- Covey, Stephen, "7 Habits of Highly Effective People", Free Press, 1989
- Denning and Dunham, "The Innovator's Way," MIT Press, 2010
- Drucker, "The New Realities," Harper & Row, 1989
- Drucker, "The Effective Executive," Harper Business, Rev Edition 2006
- Drucker, "Post-Capitalist Society," HarperBusiness, 1993
- Drucker, "Management Challenges for the 21st Century," HarperBusiness, 1999
- Drucker, "The Essential Drucker," HarperBusiness, 2001
- Epictetus, "The Complete Works of Epictetus", Indep. Pub. 2017
- Fussell, "One Mission: How Leaders Build a Team of Teams," Portfolio/Penguin, 2017
- Galllup Organization, "First Break All the Rules", Gallup Press, 2016
- Gladwell, Malcolm, "Talking to Strangers", Little, Brown & Co 2019
- Grant, Adam, "Originals," Viking 2016
- Greene, Robert, "The 48 Laws of Power", Profile Books, 1999
- Godin, Seth, "The Purple Cow", Portfolio, 2003

- Goleman, Daniel, "Emotional Intelligence", Bantman Rev Ed, 2006
- Goleman, "Primal Leadership," Harvard Business School Press, 2016
- Goleman, "Working with Emotional Intelligence," Bantam Books, 1998
- Heath and Heath, "Decisive," Crown Business, 2013
- Heath and Heath, "The Power of Moments," Simon & Schuster, 2017
- Hesselbein and Shinseki, "Be-Know-Do," Jossey-Bass, 2004
- Machiavelli, "The Prince", Indep. Pub. 2020
- Napoleon Hill, "Think and Grow Rich", Chartwell Books 2015
- Hougaard and Carter, "The Mind of the Leader," Harvard Business Review, 2018
- Keller, Gary, "The One Thing", Bard Press, 2013
- Kofman, Fred; "Conscious Business," Sounds True, 2013
- Kofman, Fred; "The Meaning Revolution," Currency, 2018
- Krogerus, "The Decision Book", WW Norton and Co., 2018
- Maxwell, John, "The 21 Laws of Leadership," Harper Collins, 2007
- Pikkety, Thomas, "Capital and Ideology", Belknap Press 2020
- Pink, Daniel, "Drive", Riverhead Books, 2009
- Plato, "Five Dialogues", Hackett Pub, 2002
- Sinck, Simon, "Start with why", Portfolio, 2009
- Sinek, Simon, "The Infinite Game", Portfolio, 2019

- Stone, Douglas, Bruce Patton, Sheil Heen, "Difficult Conversations", Penguin Books, 2010
- Sun Tzu, "The Art of War", Littl 1994
- Vaynerchuk, Gary, "Crushing It," Harper Business 2018
- Willink and Babin, "Extreme Ownership," St. Martin's Press, 2015
- Zenger & Folkman, "The Extraordinary Leader," McGraw-Hill, 2002

# ACKNOWLEDGEMENTS

To all the thousands of participants in my trainings from more than 40 countries on 5 continents.

To Raquel Rubio for helping me put all these ideas into shape.

To all the team of Cefne, Center For Negotiation, for our daily work.

To all the leaders, who taught me the techniques of leadership.

To my fellow university professors for our exchanges on these subjects.

To the next leaders to become after reading this book.

To all of you,

Thank you.

Printed in Germany
By Books On Demand
Legal deposit: June 2021

© Emerit Publishing – June 2021

ISBN ISBN 978-2-35940-027-4
97, rue Nollet
75017 Paris
http:///www.emerit-publishing.com